I am so grateful for this delightful and accessible introduction to Augustine, one of the most fascinating figures of Christian history. Here is the wonder and challenge of the Christian faith through Augustine's most personal of writings, skilfully interpreted to show how our most human struggles and longings can bring us to the love of God.

Revd Angela Tilby, Canon Emeritus of Christ Church, Oxford

The Bible Reading Fellowship
15 The Chambers, Vineyard
Abingdon OX14 3FE
brf.org.uk

The Bible Reading Fellowship (BRF) is a Registered Charity (233280)

ISBN 978 0 85746 713 3
First published 2019
10 9 8 7 6 5 4 3 2 1 0

Acknowledgements
Unless otherwise acknowledged, scripture quotations are taken from The New Revised Standard Version of the Bible, Anglicised edition, copyright © 1989, 1995 by the Division of Christian Education of the National Council of the Churches of Christ in the United States of America. Used by permission. All rights reserved.

Scripture quotation marked NIV is taken from the Holy Bible, New International Version (Anglicised edition) copyright © 1979, 1984, 2011 by Biblica. Used by permission of Hodder & Stoughton Publishers, a Hachette UK company. All rights reserved. 'NIV' is a registered trademark of Biblica. UK trademark number 1448790.

Every effort has been made to trace and contact copyright owners for material used in this resource. We apologise for any inadvertent omissions or errors, and would ask those concerned to contact us so that full acknowledgement can be made in the future.

A catalogue record for this book is available from the British Library

Printed and bound by CPI Group (UK) Ltd, Croydon CR0 4YY.

Augustine's Life of Prayer, Learning and Love

Lessons for Christian living

Cally Hammond

For the Chapel Clerks of Caius College:
I thank you for your service to our Christian community –
you have made time for me to write this book –
and let me share Augustine with you.

Contents

Introduction

Back when Christianity was still a young religion, a boy was born in north Africa who would grow up to be one of the greatest and most influential Christian thinkers who ever lived. He asked all the hard questions, and he answered them in ways that are still convincing today. He faced temptations and distractions, and he struggled within himself: he was afraid of being laughed at for his faith, but he was also desperate to be done with his old selfish lifestyle, which he was sick of but didn't know how to let go. At the same time as working out what he believed and how to live his faith, he had to earn a living and look after his family and exist somehow in a world that was much more interested in money, success and celebrity than in goodness, service of others and love of God.

Some things don't change! Even though he lived 17 centuries ago, his problems were not much different from ours. So as we learn about him, we can be sure to learn about ourselves at the same time.

There are lots of books that tell the life story of Augustine. This is not one of them. I've put some suggestions at the end of the book for those who want to look deeper into his life and his world. This book is about how he became a Christian – the problems he faced and the doubts he struggled with – and how he made sense of his belief in God and shared it with other people. It is about how he learned to read the Bible and pray. And it is about the word which is at the heart of his Christian life – *love*. Finally, it is about how he can help us, the Christians of today, to become wiser, kinder and more prayerful too.

I'm starting this journey of exploration with only a brief description of his background. He lived some 1,600 years ago (AD 354–430), mostly in north Africa, and he was brought up and educated to be a public speaker. His mother was a Christian, but his father wasn't (though he converted just before he died). After his conversion to Christian faith, he went on to be a famous preacher and teacher – probably the most famous Christian of his time. But his path to discipleship was a rocky one.

He tells us a lot about himself in his best-known book, *Confessions*. It tells the tale of someone who grew up hungry for – well, what? Hungry for something, that's for sure. Hungry for wisdom and understanding, but also hungry for praise and admiration. He was desperate to make sense of his life, but also to understand how all humanity fitted into God's plan. He longed for certainty, but he longed for people's respect and admiration too. He wanted to be wise, but mainly because it would impress others not because it would make his relationship with God better. Being valuable to God was not as important to him, in those early days, as being respected by other people. He wanted to enjoy all the good things in life, but he also knew that possessions are a snare and a distraction. And he had no idea, to start with, how to cope with these conflicting aims.

If all this makes you think, 'Hang on, Augustine sounds just like me,' you are in good company. The reason why people still read him, still study and admire him, is that he got deeper than anyone else (since Bible times) into the mystery of God's love for us, and ours for God. I'm writing this book because that is what happened to me. I began by studying Augustine's writings. I have ended up praying his words, preaching his ideas and encouraging everyone I can to get to know him for themselves. But that is not an easy thing to do when he lived so long ago and wrote in Latin. And some of his ideas have been taken up and developed in ways that are not so helpful. I'll come back to that later.

In the first few chapters of this book, I am going to look at some of the stages in Augustine's discipleship as he himself describes them in the *Confessions*. I'm not doing this to give you historical background, but rather to hold up a mirror, because at every turn, as Augustine tells you about *him*self, you will keep finding *your*self.

This is reassuring. It tells us that Augustine is not a model of Christian perfection, not someone we aspire to imitate only to fall short. The story he tells in the *Confessions* is not like any other autobiography, because he isn't telling it to the reader; he's telling it to God. In fact, the whole book is perhaps the longest prayer *ever*. He talks to God in the same way Moses did: 'the Lord used to speak to Moses face to face, *as one speaks to a friend*' (Exodus 33:11). This is where our journey with Augustine will begin: eavesdropping (with his encouragement) on a private conversation between himself and God. Later, we will learn from his conversation with God how to talk to God ourselves – and, more importantly, how to listen to God when he speaks to us.

Once we are, like Augustine, clearer about the fact that we do talk with God, and hear him respond, we will tackle another foundation of the faith – how to read the Bible. Augustine was one of the first people to ask, 'How should we read it?' We could put that another way, by asking why the Bible isn't like any other book. Here, too, Augustine's story is one of struggle to understand for himself, and then to help others understand. Reading the Bible with Augustine will not be a sterile search for facts; it will be like falling in love. The more we learn, the greater our love becomes. And by falling in love with God, we will find that talking to him in prayer is easy, and brings us the joy and peace we long for.

From Augustine's story a picture begins to emerge. Human beings have an instinctive yearning for God, which needs nurture and support. Fellow Christians ('the church') are there for us, showing us the way. They can show us how to read the Bible and make sense of it. With this support, we can begin to say some things about God himself – who he is, what he is like, why he makes himself known through his Son Jesus and through the Holy Spirit. And when we have worked through all that, we will be ready to let Augustine lead us into our own conversation with God, so that we can learn to speak with the one 'who made us for himself', so that 'our hearts are restless until they rest in him'.

In each chapter of the book I have let Augustine speak directly in his own words (using my own translation). You will quickly get to know the man himself: passionate, impetuous, dissatisfied with himself, hungry for knowledge, eager for love. And you will soon see why we should be eager to learn from his example, because then our faith will be enriched by his honesty, his curiosity and, above all, his enthusiasm for a real and deep relationship with God.

I have ended each chapter with some questions, whether for discussion in a group or personal reflection, and with a prayer drawn from Augustine's writings. I hope that you will find these helpful and that they will encourage you to discover more about this remarkable Christian and about your own faith.

Bible passage for reflection

Job answered the Lord:

'I know that you can do all things,
    and that no purpose of yours can be thwarted.
"Who is this that hides counsel without knowledge?"
Therefore I have uttered what I did not understand,
    things too wonderful for me, which I did not know.
"Hear, and I will speak;
    I will question you, and you declare to me."
I had heard of you by the hearing of the ear,
    but now my eye sees you.

JOB 42:1–5

For many Christians, faith means a battle within themselves not to listen to the questioning voice within them that wants answers, that pleads to understand God's ways. Job shows us that not only it is all right to ask questions of God, it is good and proper for us to do so. What is more, we have been given reassurance that we have within ourselves the capacity to see God and that, if we are able to admit our human frailty and confess God's divine power, he will bless us as we search deeper into his truth. This is what Augustine does, and in following his example we shall be able to open ourselves to the kind of faith, hope and love that characterised him.

Questions

1 Which is more important, our duty to family, friends, colleagues and society or our duty to God? Why?
2 Is it wrong to have doubts about our faith?
3 Why do we care so much about what other people think of us?
4 Is talking with God difficult – and if it is, why has God made it so?
5 Who in your life has been a key Christian inspiration to help you in your faith?

Prayer

Lord God, you have made us for yourself,
and our hearts are restless until they rest in you.
Teach us to live this life as travellers on a journey,
not seeking an abiding home
until we come to our Father's house,
with all its many rooms;
so that there we may lay down,
and find our home, our rest. Amen

1

Augustine's journey towards faith

On one level every human story is the same: we are born, we live and we die. On another level, every human story is different: we are born into wealth or poverty, peace or war, nurture or exploitation, education or ignorance, conformism or rebellion. Our identities are made up of a mixture of factors – genes, parental influence, peer pressure, public goals and private dreams.

Augustine's story is no different. He belongs in history, his own time, as we do in ours. But he also belongs to all time, because for 1,600 years people have been meeting him through his writings, listening to him and finding him to be a reliable guide for Christian discipleship. Few could be more aware than he was that life is limited and that our human vision and understanding are partial and imperfect. But he was also convinced that for faithful Christians the story of one life can be the story of every life. And so, in his early years as an adult Christian, he sits down to write his *Confessions*. What we find out about him in this chapter comes from that book. It is so small compared to some of his other works, but so massive in terms of its influence and power and the effect it has on almost everyone who reads it.

We can't look at the whole story in detail, so instead I have selected for us to explore together some key moments in Augustine's life up to the time of his conversion. These are moments that show us universal human experiences and give voice to universal questions:

What is sin really about? Why do so many people live their life in fear? How is it that our dreams and our reality fail to match up to each other? What does it mean to become a Christian, to repent and to be baptised? They are all only moments, only fragments of a life, but they are moments common to many of us. Looking at these moments will help us get to grips with the power of Augustine's faith and with his potential to inspire faith in us and in others. This is essential before we turn to the difficult questions of ideas and beliefs about God (what some Christians call 'theology'). Understanding the man will give us the confidence to learn from him and to tackle new ways of praying that perhaps always seemed way beyond us. It could be a rollercoaster ride!

Augustine was very clever. He knew it, too. But being so clever did not make him happy. Instead he could not understand why his being intelligent didn't help him live his life better. He used his cleverness to win praise from people instead of seeking God's approval. But he knew their praise was worthless, even though he was desperate to win such admiration. He knew that people were really only judging him according to what they saw on the surface, not according to the deep-down reality of his confused, disordered self. He couldn't help but notice how often people condemned trivial faults in others, but didn't worry about their own serious character flaws or abusive behaviour. Being a fundamentally honest person, Augustine knew he too was guilty of such hypocrisy:

> In schoolboy games I was desperate to excel, and strove to win, even if it meant cheating. I was determined not to let others cheat me, and denounced them harshly if I spotted it, but I was doing the exact same thing to them! If I was caught in the act, I chose to get angry rather than to admit the truth. So much for the innocence of youth. There is no such thing, Lord!

It is hard to read that and not think of cheating scandals in sport, such as the case of cyclist Lance Armstrong. Such attitudes are constant down the years. So is the Christian challenge to them – to be honest, whatever the cost; to put truth before personal vanity. There is also the Christian belief, rooted in the apostle Paul's equally hard-won life experience, that sometimes to lose is to win. Augustine comes to see that childhood is not a time of innocence that is gradually corrupted as life goes on; instead, weakness is part of human nature from the beginning:

> Human failings are the same from the childhood time of carers and teachers, trivia and playtimes, as in the adult transition to citizenship, work and money – they are exactly the same! But more severe punishments take the place of discipline fit for children.

Some people think that Christianity is obsessed with sin. That is not true, but sin is a vital part of understanding our relationship with God. Unless we are honest about our failings, we cannot make any progress in that relationship. Augustine was firmly convinced that we are responsible for our own failings; we cannot shuffle off responsibility by blaming them on upbringing or circumstances. Somehow, we have to accept that they are part of who we are. Only then can we move forward and begin to live life with the freedom of the gospel.

Admitting our sinfulness is liberating! Once we have confessed the worst, we can get to work on becoming who God would have us be. This is the process Augustine shows us in *Confessions*. In one way, it is like a long riff on Paul's experience in the New Testament. A move away from the kind of faith that is all about judgement and repression, to faith which is 'the glorious liberty of the children of God'.

No one, before Augustine, had tried to express what it means, what it feels like from the inside, to be a human being, from birth and childhood into adulthood – to be aware of our own existence, governed by conscience, questioning, conflicted and inspired in equal measure. Arguably, no one has done it better since. Even when he is explaining the problem of sin and how we fall short of God's ideal, he can also see how closely his failings and his talents are bound together. And vitally, he comes back again and again to that small inner voice that challenges the louder voices of temptation and distraction in his life – remember that, as usual in *Confessions*, he is talking to God:

> I was alive and self-aware, and able to protect my sense of self. My wholeness was a trace of your mystical unity, which I was part of. Some inner consciousness guarded the purity of my senses; and I delighted in truth.

Within him, as within each one of us, there is a self-awareness and an inner voice. These things connect us to God, who is beyond all that we can imagine. If we can only learn to listen to that inner voice, it will soon become clear that, what really delights us, above all else, is the truth. Because nothing can be really beautiful or worthwhile unless it is also true – and that includes God. He has to be more than a noble idea; it is God's living reality, his truth, that gives meaning to our own.

In our modern world, many people have turned away from religious faith. Instead they turn towards themselves and look within to find meaning. Like Augustine, they are aware of themselves, sometimes as individuals, sometimes as part of some wider identity, such as nationality. But cutting God out of the picture means that they cannot see themselves as *gifted* with talents and abilities, because they do not believe that there is anyone doing the giving. The missing aspect, which gives such strength to the Christian view of human life, is *gratitude*. Christians sometimes give this a specifically religious label, 'thanksgiving', but the word 'gratitude' is more helpful, because it shows us how all that is best in us comes from what God has given and not from what we can achieve for ourselves. Also, because it is understood by believers and non-believers alike, it shows that the same instinct is there in all of us. We may not believe in the God who made us, but he believes in us.

There is no Christian virtue, except forgiveness, more powerful than gratitude as a way of helping us draw close to God. This is what Augustine is trying to express when he tells God how he feels about him, and how he got confused between God and the things God has made, mixing up creator and creation:

> Surely a living creature like myself is something completely wonderful. But all my qualities are gifts from my God. I did not give them to myself. They are good, and I am the sum of all their parts. So the one who made me is good… and I rejoice in him for all the good things of which I consisted even in childhood. My sin consisted in seeking pleasure, inspiration, truth not in God himself but in the things God has made – things like me myself. As a result, I tumbled headlong into distress.

It is difficult to say anything about Augustine's understanding of sin without mentioning what he calls 'original' or 'birth' sin. He used it as a term to explain why no perfect human being has ever been born (save one, who was also truly divine – Jesus). I will be saying more about that later in the book. For now, we can simply say that it is a way of making sense of the plain fact that, as Paul puts it, *we do not do the right we want to do, but the wrong that we do not want to do, that is what we do*. We do not begin perfect in babyhood and get gradually corrupted by a sinful world eroding our goodness – like silver plating wearing off to expose base metal beneath. We are born human, which is to say frail and fallible, and we go on that way, because that is what being human really means.

There is a famous story in *Confessions* that helps us to understand human sin and frailty; Augustine tells it precisely because he knows that it looks trivial, silly, unimportant. Yet it sums up the whole truth of why our restless hearts are always searching for a way home to God. It isn't a story of grand sin. Augustine was not a Herod, a Judas or a Pontius Pilate, not a child murderer, betrayer or coward. He doesn't hurt anyone by what he does. He is not noticeably damaged by it himself. It seems to be an incident that has no cost or consequence and therefore no real significance. But we shall soon see that this is far from the case!

> There was a pear tree near to our vineyard, laden with fruit that was neither attractive nor tasty. We set out in the dead of night – a gang of good-for-nothing youths – to steal its fruit. We carried off loads, not to eat ourselves but for throwing to pigs (we did eat a few, as what we were doing was enjoyable because it was forbidden).

> Look, O God, and see my heart, see my heart! For you had mercy on it. How was it that I became a wrongdoer for nothing? It was loathsome and I loved it. Human friendship is sweetened by a precious bond, forging unity out of many souls. Yet even in pursuit of these good things, sin gains an entrance. The pears were attractive, but my poor soul did not desire them. I had plenty of better fruit at home; I plucked these only for the sake of thieving. I threw away what I had stolen. I feasted on my own wickedness. If one morsel of fruit passed my lips, it was sin that sweetened it.

> Now, O Lord my God, what was it about the theft that gave me pleasure? Had I been alone, I would not have done it (I remember thinking so at the time). So what I loved about it was participating with others in doing what I did. My pleasure was not in the pears; it was in the actual sin that a fellowship of sinners committed together. Out of a lark came an eagerness to do harm, a taste for inflicting losses on others without myself gaining anything. Once someone says, 'Come on, let's do it,' it is shameful to be anything but shameless.

> I deviated from you, I have wandered from the path, my God. In my teens I was too inconstant in your steadfastness, and I made myself into a barren land.

When Augustine tells this trivial anecdote of his teenage years, and shares his thoughts on it with God, and with us, trying to make sense of what it means to be a human being, he is looking back after ten years as an adult Christian. His faith is not new; its roots are not shallow. He has spent a long time thinking about the mystery of faith, and what God wants of him and of all of us. And he is honest and realistic about human sin. People distort the truth; they deny God; they prefer the broad way to destruction, not the narrow path that leads to life (Matthew 7:13).

Our default setting all too often is to do what is easy rather than what is right. Many Christians would stop at this point and make the Christian message mainly one of warning and denouncing. We are wrong, we are bad, we let God down and we betray his trust. Augustine does not do this. Instead he takes the harder path, trying to find answers to questions other people hadn't even thought of asking. It wasn't until I read *Confessions* that I really started to ask myself how we can actually know anything about God at all. Perhaps this is a question you're now ready to ask yourself. The fact is, we *experience* God long before we try to know things about him. We reach out to him in wordless prayer, or go to church and worship, or share faith with fellow Christians, and we feel our hearts strangely warmed. Then we start to puzzle out what it all means, and how we have come to have these insights into our own nature – how we come to be convinced that we are not alone and that we are created, redeemed and sustained by God.

Augustine shows us the answer to this puzzle. Given the sinful state in which we live, ignoring God, disobeying him, shutting him out, how could we ever have any knowledge about him in the first place – unless *he put it there for us to find*? Our search for God, our 'restlessness' (to use Augustine's word), our 'hearts aflame for the one' who made us (his words again): all are prompted by that sense, deep within us, that God simply *is*. Who, what, how, why God is – all this comes later. But *that* God is, is our starting point. So we can take our belief in God for granted, and often do – without stopping to ask how it is that we can even think such thoughts, have such ideas, unless God somehow made us a field ready for sowing. The seeds of faith are already germinating in the field of our hearts without any effort on our part.

It is odd to think that over all these centuries, from Bible times up to today, we still all face the same experience. Basically, it comes down to being tempted to give up on God in favour of some easier way, being afraid to do the right thing for fear of being judged. Most of all, making wrongdoing easier by not doing it alone. The story of the pears brings the whole thing into focus. Each one of us always has a choice; but being with others when they choose wrong and sin makes it harder for us (why?) to say no ourselves, and makes it easier for us to join in and go astray. We are not alone. Our weaknesses are part of what it is for all of us to be human; and we must face those weaknesses as Augustine eventually did. Honestly. Saying sorry. Determining not to be a prisoner of the past but accepting that we are free to choose what is good.

One of the biggest issues faced by today's Christians is sexual morality. There is so much disagreement about what is right, normal and good. You might think that it was all much clearer and simpler in earlier times, but that isn't so. Augustine was brought up in a society in which different customs and beliefs clashed all the time – just like our society, in fact. One thing he was 100% clear about, though, was that for a Christian, sex outside marriage was wrong. And those who committed that sin were condemned. And that was a big problem for him. He had done the usual thing for a young man from his background and chosen a woman to be his bed-sharer ('concubine') – a girlfriend, we would probably call her. She came from a lower social class, which in those days meant he was legally unable to marry her. They lived together, faithful to one another, for years. They even had a son together and called him Adeodatus, which means 'Given by God'. But the customs of his time meant that if he wanted to become a Christian, he would have to give her up. And he could not bring himself to do it.

This was one great obstacle in his way – how he could commit himself to Christ, when he thought he was incapable of living without a sexual partner. But this was only part of the problem. In fact, it wasn't the real problem at all; it was the *excuse*. In other words, as long as he could keep saying, 'I can't become a Christian because I could never live up to the Christian ideal of chastity,' he would not have to respond to the insistent voice of God within him, calling him to come home. He didn't want the upset, the change to his pattern of life. He didn't want other people to laugh at him either. This was a constant anxiety. Right from his childhood, he had been afraid of people laughing at him, mocking him. And that fear of others' scorn never really went away.

Most of us are influenced by our families and friends, for better or worse. We feel that they know us best, so we respect their judgement. Augustine had a close childhood friend whose opinion he valued, and they loved one another dearly, as friends do. One day the friend fell ill, and his illness made Augustine stop and think. Where would his friend go if he died? To heaven? To hell? To nothingness? They had shared everything as they grew up together, but now his friend (he never tells us his name) was about to go where Augustine could not follow. He had fallen unconscious, and while he was unconscious he had been baptised. For a little while, he recovered, and Augustine tried to get him to go back to their old ways – laughing at baptism as if it were nothing, making light of faith. But the friend had changed. He didn't feel that way any more. Baptism had liberated him from all that childish preoccupation with other people's opinions. He no longer cared what other people thought of him or how they might judge him. He was a Christian now.

Soon after being baptised, his friend died, and Augustine was plunged into a terrible grief. The grief was compounded by the choking fear that overcame Augustine, as he grew more and more anxious about death and judgement. Separation from his dear friend was bad enough – how, he asked, could the rest of the world go on living, as if nothing had happened? He was torn between two kinds of hopelessness. On the one hand there was the possibility that after death came oblivion, nothingness. And on the other was the equally terrifying possibility that there *would* be life after death, but that he would be excluded from it because of not being a Christian himself.

Just as with sexual desire, so with human love and affection: what was made by God, and so was good, was being corrupted by Augustine's refusal to put God at the centre instead of himself. In this state of utter despair, he describes what we would nowadays call 'alienation', a feeling of being isolated from the community, the companionship of other people and social groups, and being separated from all that is good:

> My soul should've been lifted up to you, Lord. It should've been healed. I knew it, but I didn't want to; I didn't have the strength. This was because to me you didn't exist; you were just an imaginary being. I was in an unhappy place where I could not bear to stay, but couldn't leave either. Where could my heart flee, to escape from my heart? Where could I flee, to escape from myself? Where could I get to, without ending up pursuing myself?

Augustine's mind was like a wheel spinning on a bike that has fallen to the ground – going round and round but getting nowhere fast. His own thoughts, instead of helping him through the grief of his friend's death, worsened that grief.

What strikes me now, as I reread those words of his, is how *strong* his mind was. How fiercely he fought against the pull of his heart which was trying to return to God. He wanted to be self-reliant, in control of his own intelligence, able to govern his emotions, but he couldn't. Something was in the way. Something invisible but huge.

That something was pride. 'Pride' is a word like 'thanksgiving' – it has a special meaning for Christians. We use it to describe that state of self-reliance in which we try to do without God, in which we ourselves take credit for the gifts given to us, instead of acknowledging the one who made us. Augustine was like many people today: he wanted to find a path, a way to live life well, but he wanted to find it for himself and live it on his own terms. He was afraid of others looking down on him; he wanted a way of life that impressed people, not one they would laugh at.

Becoming a Christian wasn't going to impress anyone. Instead Augustine joined a trendy alternative religious movement called Manichaeism. This had a lot going for it that appealed to him at that time of his life. It claimed to offer a way of understanding how the world was made. It explained good and evil as being two forces locked in endless conflict. Throughout his life, Augustine was interested in the origin of evil, so this aspect of Manichaeism had a particularly strong appeal. And crucially, it offered two levels of commitment. There was an inner circle, which lived according to the highest, purest ideals, but there was also a lower level of membership, in which you got the benefits of the teaching and philosophy, plus all the affirmation that comes with being part of the group, but without having to give up sex and other physical pleasures such as food and drink.

Perfect. Or so he thought. He spent nine years as part of this group, always on that lower, less-demanding level of commitment. He was still too proud to become a Christian, too afraid to let go of physical appetites, and determined not to admit that he was not the controller of his own destiny.

Augustine's membership of this group drove a wedge between him and his mother. She was a Christian, and wanted nothing to do with what she saw as ungodly ways. She kept praying for him to find his way to true faith. It must have been hard to live through – for both of them, and for his brother and sister, too. Anyone who has let go of their parents' way of believing to embrace faith in their own way will recognise how hard this must have been for the whole family. But God was at work in it all. Augustine and his mother (Monnica) both had to endure that time of unhappiness. There were no shortcuts to the shared Christian faith that brought them both such joy later. The way of the cross was not easy then, any more than it is now.

Bible passage for reflection

The fear of the Lord is the beginning of knowledge;
    fools despise wisdom and instruction…

My child, if you accept my words
    and treasure up my commandments within you,
making your ear attentive to wisdom
    and inclining your heart to understanding;
if you indeed cry out for insight,
    and raise your voice for understanding;
if you seek it like silver,
    and search for it as for hidden treasures –
then you will understand the fear of the Lord
    and find the knowledge of God.
For the Lord gives wisdom;
    from his mouth come knowledge and understanding;
he stores up sound wisdom for the upright;
    he is a shield to those who walk blamelessly,
guarding the paths of justice
    and preserving the way of his faithful ones.
PROVERBS 1:7; 2:1–8

The book of Proverbs is all about wisdom – not human wisdom, but God's wisdom. It is frank, straightforward advice on how to live well, rather than abstract theorising about the meaning of goodness, love or justice. Augustine was inspired in his youth to search for wisdom, but he looked in the wrong places and could not find what he was seeking, until he heard God's word to him, and his life changed forever.

Questions

1 Do we become Christians because we fear God, or because we love God?
2 Thinking of your own family background, what have you learned from it about how to approach God?
3 Have you ever done something wrong for the sheer thrill of misbehaving or rebelling (don't feel that you have to answer this question if it makes you feel uncomfortable)?
4 Does it matter what other people (Christian or non-Christian) think of us when we declare our faith for the first time?

Prayer

Lord God, you know how we fall short of our ideals:
how discontented we can be
with the life we have chosen for ourselves;
and yet how afraid of change, even change that sets us free.
Strengthen our trust that we can rest secure in you;
so that we no longer feel a need to flee,
or to escape from the old self that weighs us down.
Then call us to your side, to abide with you always,
in this life and the next. Amen

2

Conversion, baptism and getting to grips with the Bible

For those of us who have always believed in God and always been aware of his presence in our lives, it can be difficult to understand those who have a 'conversion experience'. But for everyone who believes, whether or not they have a conversion experience, there must come a time when they have to turn private faith into public faith. Some decide to be baptised or confirmed. Some come forward after their conversion and offer testimony, confessing their faith, in public worship. Others show that public commitment by choosing a life of Christian service. It can be confusing when there are so many ways of showing that you are a Christian. Is one way better than another? Is being 'born again' the only real way, or is 'quiet conviction' a better path?

One thing that confuses all sorts of Christians is the nature of the change that happens when we say that we are believers. We make the mistake of thinking that becoming a Christian is all about *making a decision*, as if it was our choice, made in the thinking part of us, a matter of facts and knowledge. In reality, although facts and knowledge matter, and matter a lot, when it comes to becoming a Christian, it is not something we decide or do; it happens *to* us. And it happens in God's good time, not when we think it would be convenient for it to happen.

This is important, because it takes all the pressure off us. We don't need to worry about whether we are good enough or wise enough. We only need to let go of our pride and our need for control, and let God set us free to follow. What comes to us through this letting go of self is the deepest liberation imaginable, a feeling almost beyond words. As one Christian in earlier times put it (and how his words touch my heart and express my experience), 'I glory in nothing so much as that I am a Christian: that your name is called upon me. O my God, though I die, yet will I put my trust in you.'

It matters that we understand this now, because otherwise we can't make sense of what Augustine tells us in his *Confessions*. From the way he tells his own story, it is obvious that right from the start he always wanted God. He was always looking for him. This makes it hard to understand why, in the circumstances, he didn't just say, 'I am a Christian.' Why couldn't he make the decision and just tell everyone openly what he'd decided? Once he gave up his trendy alternative religion, Manichaeism, surely that was the moment to be born again? But that is not what happened. Instead, he had to undergo two experiences. The conversion of his heart (his emotions, feelings and soul) did not happen until after the conversion of his mind (his intelligence and understanding). And that brings us to how he discovered the Bible.

When Augustine was a young man, the Bible for him was not a guide book. It was not a help, a precious source of wisdom and strength. It was a stumbling block. He turned to it for guidance, as truth-seekers always have, and as we Christians still do. But he didn't know *how* to read it. And when he tried to read it, he found that it was complicated, mystifying, full of stuff he didn't understand. He couldn't make head or tail of it. How many people try the same thing nowadays, and with the same result? They decide to read it, determine to do so 'cover to cover', quickly get stuck, struggle – and soon give up. It takes years of reading and thinking and praying before the Bible comes fully into focus for a Christian. And before we understand it in all its parts.

Of course, there are many, very many, passages where the word of God speaks to us plainly and directly:

- 'God is love' (1 John 4:8)
- 'In everything do to others as you would have them do to you' (Matthew 7:12)
- 'Father, I have sinned against heaven and before you; I am no longer worthy to be called your son' (Luke 15:18–19)
- 'Come to me, all you that are weary and are carrying heavy burdens, and I will give you rest' (Matthew 11:28)
- 'The kingdom of God has come near; repent, and believe in the good news' (Mark 1:15)
- 'Faith, hope, and love abide, these three; and the greatest of these is love' (1 Corinthians 13:13)
- 'The one who calls you is faithful' (1 Thessalonians 5:24).

But we have to do a lot of reading before we can learn where to find those passages. And we often get bogged down in other stuff, more difficult stuff, and the detail seems utterly beyond us. This can be very off-putting to those who are new to faith.

You won't be surprised by now to discover that Augustine was in exactly the same boat. He wanted to read the Bible; he wanted to learn what it said and understand what it meant. But he tried, and he couldn't, not all by himself, anyway. Then he did something sensible, something many of us do in the same situation – he searched for a Christian more mature in faith to help him. In his case, the person he settled on was the bishop of Milan, a man called Ambrose. Augustine admired Ambrose very much. Ambrose was distinguished and clever, and Augustine instinctively looked up to him and respected him. Here, he felt, was someone he could do business with, someone on his own level. He still had a lot to learn!

Augustine looked at Ambrose's way of life and admired it. It was simple. Ambrose devoted most of his time to study and worship. When Augustine heard him preach, he found many of the problems that beset him dealt with and his questions answered. Everything was beginning to make sense. It was as if Ambrose was a lens to help bring his faith into sharp focus. Augustine particularly wanted Ambrose's help in making sense of the Bible. He asked for advice, and the advice he was given was 'Go and read the prophet Isaiah.'

I have often wondered why Ambrose told him to start there. Perhaps it was because Isaiah gives the clearest prophecy in the whole of the Old Testament about the coming of Christ (Isaiah 7:14), and it was Christ that Augustine was looking for. Nowadays, if someone asks me for help reading the Bible, I tell them to start with Mark's gospel, because it is short, clear and compelling. It is the simplest place to meet Jesus and start getting to know him. I know of a brilliant scientist who set out to disprove the Bible by reading the gospels, was utterly confounded by the goodness of Jesus, and changed his mind about the Christian faith from that time forward. We could almost say that Jesus is his own best advert. But Isaiah is a much harder book to make sense of, so how did Augustine get on with following Ambrose's advice?

If Augustine's faith was just something in a story, he would have gone off to read Isaiah, and everything would have worked out fine. He would have found the answers he was seeking, just like that. Instead, it was real life, like our real-life experiences of reading the Bible, and things worked out rather differently:

> I wrote to Ambrose, to tell him of my former sins and my present intentions. I asked for his advice on which of the Bible's many books I ought to read, to prepare me for baptism. He told me to read the prophet Isaiah. I think this was because Isaiah foretells the gospel and the call to non-Jewish people. But when I read it, I did not understand it. I expected that the whole of Isaiah would be the same: so I put it to one side, intending to try again later, when I was more familiar with the Bible.

This makes me smile. Here is one of the greatest Christian thinkers ever, telling us he couldn't make head or tail of this Bible book. His honesty is refreshing; it ought to cheer us up, so that we too feel it is all right to say, 'I don't get it.' Have you ever had a similar experience, being told to read something, being promised that it will help – and then instead found it utterly unhelpful? If so, you will be able to sympathise with Augustine. The plain fact is that a lot of the Bible is dark and mysterious, and we can spend a lifetime getting to understand it. Augustine did exactly that. The whole of the rest of his life was taken up with studying scripture. Again like all of us, he had books that were his favourites, which spoke to him more clearly and appealingly about God and Christ. He was always fascinated by Genesis, especially the opening chapters, with their exploration of good and evil. He loved the psalms, preached on them often and quoted them constantly. He loved the gospels and letters of the New Testament, of course.

Here is an interesting exercise we can try for ourselves. Ask yourself, 'If I could only rescue five of the 66 books of the Bible, which would I choose?' Thinking about this for myself, I realised I would have to have a gospel, or perhaps two – John and either Matthew or Luke. I could not live as a worshipping Christian without the Psalms. I think (despite Augustine's experience) I would have to save Isaiah, and that would leave me only one more choice. As I write, I'm still stuck between Romans and 1 Corinthians. Everyone will have their own answer to this impossible question, of course, but it does help us to see clearly how some parts of the Bible in practice (though not in theory) matter more to us than others. I can't honestly say that I would miss Ezra, Nehemiah or Chronicles; I would miss Ecclesiastes and the Song of Songs, but I know they are not fundamental to my faith in the same way that the gospels and some of the prophets are.

This is hardly surprising. The Bible is a big collection of books. All of it is the inspired word of God, but because people are different and have different needs, different parts of the Bible speak more clearly to one person than to another. And our needs change over time, as our lives change. For example, when we are blessed with children, it gives us fresh insight into what the Bible says about children, and into the story of Jesus when he was a child. When we suffer a bereavement, it may be 1 Corinthians 15, Romans 8, Revelation 21 or John 14 that stays at the forefront of our minds as we try to make sense of what we are enduring. When we are confronted with injustice, we find the Old Testament prophets give a voice to the voiceless and hope to the oppressed. If we were to suffer exile or be victims of ethnic cleansing, surely the story of Exodus would speak most clearly to our hearts – as it did to Africans sold into slavery in the USA, exploited and tyrannised by taskmasters who treated them as less than human.

Augustine was not ready to hear the message of Isaiah. I don't think he ever really got to grips with it, because other biblical books caught his attention and touched his heart more deeply. You can see this at work when he tells us about how the barrier between himself and God broke down, when his change of *mind* about Christianity became also a change of *heart*. He tells us, in *Confessions*, about two key moments when the Bible spoke directly to him – not as a piece of writing for him to analyse, discuss or research, but as the pure voice of God, the divine heart of love speaking to his human heart. In both cases, words that he had known before, and known for a long time, took on new significance because of his circumstances. That is, he experienced something familiar to almost every Christian – old words spoke to him in a new way, and when he went to the Bible in search of guidance, he found exactly what he had been looking for, because this was the moment, the 'right time', for those words to yield their full power and meaning:

> I spoke to you at length, Lord, along these lines: 'How long, Lord? Lord, how long will you be angry, forever? Do not remember our former sins any more' [Psalm 79:5, 8]. For I felt that I was in the grip of my sins. I sobbed, 'How long? How long must it be "tomorrow" and "tomorrow"? Why not "now"?' These were my words, and in grief of heart I wept bitterly.

Then, look! From the house next door, I hear a voice – I don't know whether it is a boy's or a girl's – singing some words over and over: 'Pick it up and read it, pick it up and read it!' I started to ask myself eagerly whether it was common for children to chant such words when they were playing a game. I could not recall ever having heard anything quite like it. I checked the flow of my tears and got up. I understood it as nothing short of divine providence that I was being ordered to open the book and read the first passage I came across.

This is a famous story, and for a good reason. Augustine is describing an experience that sounds familiar to many Christians. The words of scripture are speaking directly to him, to his own situation, his own difficulties. And he responds by replying in his own words, speaking straight to God, as God's word (in the Bible) has spoken first to him. At this very moment, the moment when he lets God into his life and speaks to him as we are all called to do, not as a distant and alien being but as a loving and beloved Father, God speaks back to him. And God's voice is not the sound of thunder and might, but is heard in a small voice, the voice of a child. That child's voice speaks the simplest words imaginable, 'Pick it up and read it!' These words could mean anything, to anyone. But to Augustine, in this place, at this time, they mean, 'Pick up the Bible and read it as a Christian reads it. Let it speak to you, to your mind, to your heart. Listen to what it says and act on what you hear.' In that simple phrase, 'Pick it up and read it,' if we listen properly, there is a treasure store of meaning.

At this point, Augustine had never studied the Bible properly. Like most people hovering on the edge of faith, he had dipped his toe in, and found it too difficult. But that is because he had been reading it as if it were a book like any other, not as if it were the inspired word of God, and the source of all we need for our salvation. So, what he describes is a process in which the help comes from outside ourselves; but we remain free to embrace it or refuse it, to say 'yes' to God or to shut him out and turn a deaf ear to his call.

Augustine didn't yet have an expert view of the holy books; that took years of study. But he knew in his heart that the Bible was full of wisdom and truth, and that if he engaged with it in that way, it would never let him down. He believed this partly because he had heard the story of a saint called Antony, who lived in Egypt a hundred years before his own time, who had the same experience and became a Christian monk as a result:

> I had heard of Antony, how he had been challenged by a reading from the gospel that he happened to encounter, as if what he was reading was being spoken for himself: 'Go, sell everything you possess and give to the poor, and you will have treasure in the heavens: and come, follow me!' [Matthew 19:21]. Straightaway he was converted to you.

As Augustine tells the story of this life-changing moment of conversion, we get a sense of the excitement and the relief that were flooding his being. He has asked for help, asked for answers. And the answers have come:

> In great excitement I returned to my friend, because I had left him with a copy of the letters of Paul. I snatched up the book, opened it and read silently the first chapter that my eyes lit upon: 'Not in partying and drunkenness, not in promiscuity and shamelessness, not in fighting and jealousy, but clothe yourself in the Lord Jesus Christ and make no provision for the flesh concerning its physical desires' [Romans 13:13–14].

> I didn't want or need to read further. Immediately, the end of the sentence was like a light of sanctuary poured into my heart [John 1:9]; every shadow of doubt melted away. Then I showed the passage to my friend, Alypius. He read even further on than I had looked. I did not know what came next, but it was this: 'Receive the one who is weak in faith' [Romans 14:1]. He read these words as if they applied to himself, and showed them to me.

I think many, perhaps even most, Christians have tried this for themselves, at one time or another, as a way to ask God to speak to them through his word. To open the Bible and read a verse at random, trust that it will be the right message for this situation, and then try to apply it to one's life is clearly something Christians have been doing right from the beginning.

To an outsider, it seems an odd way to make decisions; but to a believer, the fact that the Bible has been tried and tested and found to be rich in meaning and to speak into every imaginable eventuality in life – this makes it much more understandable and reasonable. It is not so much about finding an instruction and following it however irrelevant; it is more a matter of being open to possibilities beyond the reach of one's own limited capacity. Letting the Bible speak into our doubt and deliberation may have its risks, but it is at heart a sound practice.

As we have seen, getting to grips with the Bible is not always easy. Sometimes it is simple and straightforward, but at other times we have to wrestle with it and ask ourselves hard questions, just as Augustine did. But we all – Christians of the past and of today – share the belief that the Bible *will* speak if we are prepared to listen. It *can* transform our lives, as it did Augustine's. It *can* overcome our doubts and difficulties. This is not because it is a rule book, not even because it is a guidebook. Rather it is because the Bible is a *story*book – a book telling the 'old, old story' of God and his love for his people.

This was where Augustine began when he gave up reading the Bible as a student of literature would and began to let it speak to him as God's story; and from it Augustine learned that 'even the fact that I exist was a gift from you, God, to me'. This is a useful reminder that God is not disposable, a part of the package we can strip away. There is no 'outside' to God, no objective viewpoint from which to make sense of existence and being. God is above all, and through all, and in all (Ephesians 4:6; Colossians 1:16–17), so life can only ever make proper sense to us when we see it through eyes of faith.

Bible passage for reflection

'Can any of you by worrying add a single hour to your span of life? And why do you worry about clothing? Consider the lilies of the field, how they grow; they neither toil nor spin, yet I tell you, even Solomon in all his glory was not clothed like one of these. But if God so clothes the grass of the field, which is alive today and tomorrow is thrown into the oven, will he not much more clothe you – you of little faith? Therefore do not worry, saying, "What will we eat?" or "What will we drink?" or "What will we wear?" For it is the Gentiles who strive for all these things; and indeed your heavenly Father knows that you need all these things. But strive first for the kingdom of God and his righteousness, and all these things will be given to you as well.'
MATTHEW 6:27–33

There is a world of difference between what we need to live well and what we *think* we need. Jesus gives us the best advice, to save our energy for things that matter and not waste it on what is trivial or completely beyond our control. Before his conversion, Augustine would have been counted among those 'Gentiles' who strive for what is worthless and miss out on things of true value, but he had sense enough to know that he was wasting his life, and he was just beginning to perceive what he needed to pursue in place of the things he must let go of.

Questions

1 Have you had a conversion experience or conversion moment? If so, has it made being a Christian easier? If not, do you think you are missing out?
2 Can you think of an example from your own life where words from the Bible have turned you from one path to another?
3 Is there a single book of the Bible you value above all the rest?
4 Is there a single book of the Bible that you struggle with more than all the rest?
5 When Augustine tells us about hearing the child's voice, does that remind you of similar experiences of your own, finding a message from God in something apparently ordinary?

Prayer

God our Father, we long to matter,
for our lives not to pass unnoticed,
and for our needs to be met with love;
help us to be slower to speak, and readier to listen,
when we pray to you;
so that when you call us, and speak to us,
we will be ready to hear, and discover
that we are already nurtured and protected,
under the shadow of your wings. Amen

3

Augustine on debates and disagreements

By the time Augustine was born, Christianity was no longer a religion suffering from persecution and martyrdom. It was gradually becoming the official religion of the Roman empire – in other words, the official religion of the entire known world. It had been a favourite saying of Roman historians long ago that the best way for the Roman people to secure peace in domestic politics was for them to have an external threat that they could unite against. Once this external threat to Christianity evaporated, splits between groups of Christians became much more noticeable and much more damaging. Then, as now, such disagreements undermined Christians when they claimed to be peaceable and dedicated to showing others the way of love.

Augustine had all the zeal of the true convert. Like someone who has given up smoking and can't bear even the sight or smell of a cigarette, he was angry with himself for the nine wasted years spent in that fake form of faith called Manichaeism. Because of his eagerness for wisdom, combined with his lack of any firm intellectual foundation for his faith, he had fallen an easy prey to charlatans. He was determined to do what he could to help others, so that they didn't make the same mistakes he once had.

He realised how important it was to be clear about what Christians believe and what real Christianity is all about and to avoid disputes and clashes between groups of Christians, which risked endangering the gospel message by bringing the faith into disrepute. Once he became bishop of Hippo (a town in north Africa), he spent a lot of time trying to promote unity and harmony among the various Christian communities. What he did *not* do was try to disguise such disagreements by thinking up clever forms of words to include as many people as possible or to paper over differences of understanding between those Christian groups.

It would be nice to think that years ago Christians were not divided on party lines, and that they were always kind and, well, *Christian* in their behaviour to each other. But it was not so. They disagreed then, as now, about who was the right kind of Christian and about who taught the most authentic version of the faith. And because they were all firmly convinced that there was no hope for anyone to be saved unless they believed in the right kind of Christianity, the stakes were as high as they could possibly be.

Anything which fractured unity between Christians, or brought the faith into disrepute, mattered to Augustine. Maintaining unity in the church took up so much of his time in his later years that it squeezed out almost everything else. From this period of his life we have lots of writings: books of theology; books on how to understand the Bible and live the Christian life; and hundreds of letters and sermons. But the young man who fell in love with God in that garden, and described his love in his *Confessions*, seems to have faded from our sight. There are no more 'confessions' in the form of long conversations with God about faith, life and meaning; no more passionate searches for the truth of what it means to be a human being. He has a job to do now; his life is not just a matter of self-discovery and inner discernment; God has set him to labour in the vineyard, and he does so, right through the heat of the day until 'the fever of life is over, and his work is done' (John Henry Newman; see Matthew 20:1–16).

We have no way of knowing whether Augustine the bishop, the church leader and teacher, still experienced moments of ecstasy and vision in his prayers. If he did, he decided not to share them with us. I hope that he did continue to grow in prayer and closeness to God, but I suspect that combating wrong-headed forms of faith and challenging Christian misbehaviour took up so much of his time and energy that it was difficult to find time for the kind of prayer that is open-ended, difficult simply to enjoy being in God's company without thinking about the next duty, the next task. It is clear that he felt it was his duty to do this kind of debate and speak out against some misguided takes on the gospel. But I don't get the impression that he enjoyed it. He was not a natural debater who revelled in the tussles, the to and fro of argument and dialogue. He put all his effort and energy into guiding people to the truth, not scoring debating points.

Over the decades Augustine handled many different, and difficult, problems for Christians. But two particular problems came to dominate his later life: one was combating 'heresy' – in other words, debate about what counts as right belief. The other was combating 'schism' – the tendency of groups of Christians to split up into competing factions, often over apparently trivial matters. In north Africa, while he was bishop, there was a large population of Christians known as Donatists. They saw themselves as the only true Christians in the area and would have nothing to do with the rest of the Christian population, regarding them as traitors and collaborators. Even after the empire had been Christianised for decades, Donatists were suspicious of any church that had 'collaborated' (as they saw it) with the Roman authorities back in the days of persecution. The Donatists were determined to be martyrs, even if it meant provoking people into condemning them.

One of the things that gave the Donatists their strength was that sense of identity, seeing themselves as the church of the martyrs. They had a strong African identity too and were not at all keen on submitting to Roman influence, either from the bishop of Rome or from the emperor. They favoured the teachings of Cyprian, an African Christian martyred in the third century, who had declared, 'The church is the Spirit working through people of the Spirit; the church is not a collection of bishops.' They also claimed that Cyprian was on their side when he had written, 'Anyone who shatters the peace and harmony of Christ is acting against Christ. Anyone who gathers outside the Church scatters the Church of Christ. Anyone who does not keep this unity does not hold God's law, does not keep the faith of Father and Son, does not keep life and salvation.' Of course, Augustine and those in the majority party of Christians agreed with that statement too, and they also claimed the man who had said it was on their side; according to their view, it was a condemnation of the Donatists, not at all an endorsement of them!

In the end Augustine's efforts to end the schism between the Donatists and the majority of Christians failed, probably because he was trying to persuade them with wise ideas, sensible arguments and biblical teaching, while they had a more political agenda. They wanted their own identity more than they wanted to belong to the universal church, which was Augustine's understanding of what God intended for humankind, and they were more than happy to resort to violence to protect their own interests. Christianity disappeared from north Africa soon after Augustine's death, and it is hard not to conclude that the schism, that catastrophic split which drove Christians on both sides to put arguing with each other above spreading the gospel, was responsible for the ultimate silencing of the gospel message in north Africa for centuries to come.

When it came to heresy, Augustine found himself with a different type of problem, and needing different tools to fight it. Once again, though, he took on the challenge, and battled for Christian truth in a way that continues to this day – defending the true meaning of grace against a version of Christianity according to which we can *earn* our forgiveness simply by doing good, behaving well and living a decent life. Augustine was not a man to shy away from difficult questions or unattractive answers; if the Bible pointed to a hard teaching, that was that, as far as he was concerned. It was not for him to weaken the gospel or mitigate the message. This was especially true of his teaching on grace and human sin.

By the end of the fourth century, when Augustine became a leader in the church, Christians had been trying to work out what to do about sin for a long time. They believed the Bible's teaching that baptism washes away sin, but they didn't have a clue what to do about sins committed after baptism. One solution was to rebaptise people. That was eventually ruled out. Another was to delay baptism as long as possible; but it was a risky strategy – what about accidents and sudden illnesses? It was no use having saved up your 'get out of hell free' card if you never got a chance to play it. Eventually, it came to be accepted that baptism washes away sin and that it puts the baptised person where they belong, within the fold of Christ's flock, but that everyone will go on committing sins and will need to go on confessing them, in order to remain in a right relationship with God. It was becoming fashionable to dedicate your life to God through various forms of self-denial, such as depriving yourself of food, warmth or shelter. This was seen as a way of getting back to basics and wrestling with faith.

But even that good and proper aim had a downside. The downside was a belief that if you tried hard enough and lived a life of self-denial and hardship, it would be possible (in theory anyway) to live a life worthy of God. It was a form of teaching popular with some Christians, who wanted, understandably, to improve themselves and make spiritual progress. Or perhaps, less attractively, they were trying to separate themselves from other, in their opinion lesser, believers.

This form of teaching about how to live a Christian life was exemplified by a British man called Pelagius, a kind of religious guru. He and Augustine disagreed about pretty much everything that mattered when it came to grace and goodness. Pelagius was convinced that God would not have called human beings to live a moral life unless he had also given us the capacity to make that moral life a reality. Augustine, on the other hand, was equally convinced that nothing we could ever do would be adequate to earn our salvation or to ensure that we had deserved divine grace because we had tried so hard to please God. There was no room for compromise; as soon as each became aware of the other's views, the battle lines were fixed. Pelagius thought Augustine was making God an unreasonable tyrant. Augustine thought Pelagius was emptying the cross of meaning and denying the possibility of salvation – at one point he even called Pelagius 'the enemy of grace'.

People have always disagreed about questions of life and meaning, so the fact of this disagreement between Augustine and Pelagius isn't surprising in itself. All kinds of puzzles and issues were discussed in those days, just as Christians debate important issues today: the origin of evil; whether evil is a thing in itself or simply the absence of good; whether God created the world out of nothing; why God had to send his Son to die on the cross as the way of saving the human race; and so on. There were also debates about whether each person's life was mapped out in advance. Augustine used to worry about the uncertainty of human life, just like everyone does. Before he became a Christian, he had been briefly attracted by astrology and fortune-telling. Lots of people at the time, including Christians, believed in fate, a mysterious power that allocated to each person their span of life and that dictated the kind of life they would turn out to live.

Augustine came to see this fatalism as non-Christian. Instead he argued for what he called divine providence. Like the concept of fate or destiny, providence also holds that history is not random but going in a direction, but it denies the idea that human beings are without a free will. We can choose to be, or do, whatever we like. God does not make us behave in particular ways; he sets us free to make up our own mind. But at the same time, he 'foreknows', or 'foresees' (which is what providence really means), what choices we make because he does not see our lives as we do, unfolding in time. He is outside time, and to him every moment of human history, and every moment of our individual human lives, is 'now'.

Human societies, so Augustine believed, are established and dir-ected by divine providence. Human individuals are subject to forces over which they have no control and about which they have no real understanding. But God still regards them as having personal responsibility for their actions and a capacity for achieving virtue. This is hard to make sense of. At first it looks as if Augustine is arguing that God makes it impossible for people to avoid sinning or to do good, then condemns them as responsible for the sins they cannot help committing, however hard they try. Put like that, it sounds desperately unfair and even cruel.

But Augustine is not thinking in logical terms. He is trying to do justice to what he reads in scripture and what he has experienced in his own Christian journey. And what he sees, in retrospect, is that God's guiding hand was upon him but that, at the time, he knew himself also to be morally free to choose his own way and morally responsible for the choices that he made. Plenty of Christians feel this way about their faith. I do myself. It is honest, and it is realistic. Logic is not the only kind of sense that matters.

That is not to say that questions of grace (God's undeserved mercy and goodwill towards human beings) and free will are trivial. Other Christian teachers as well as Augustine saw the problems with overemphasising human freedom of choice. It is difficult for us to forget the knowledge we have nowadays and to see the problem as they saw it so long ago. The science of genetics has helped us to understand ourselves as complex combinations of inherited characteristics, on the one hand, and learned behaviours, on the other. It would be nice to think that the debate over how these two interact in people has always been restrained and polite on both sides, but in fact it has been quite the reverse – abusing the people you disagreed with was all too common.

Augustine tried to avoid such slanging matches. He was unusual in that respect and deserves all the more credit for not giving in to his less kindly feelings about those who disagreed with him. Another critic of Pelagius abused him, not for his actual teaching but for being 'fat', 'ugly', 'stupid', 'arrogant' and 'vain'. Augustine didn't sink to that level of venom. But when Pelagius read a sentence in *Confessions* that offended him, because it seemed that Augustine was denying human free will, he didn't hold back. What Augustine had said, to God, was simply this: 'Grant what you command, and command what you will.' In other words, he had been expressing his sense of the sovereignty of God, and of his own absolute duty of obedience to God. Pelagius chose to take it in the worst sense possible, and he used it to attack the man he now saw as his chief opponent: he claimed that Augustine was at heart basically still a Manichaean, teaching an eternal opposition between the equal forces of good and evil, with human beings unable to break free, incapable of avoiding sin. Augustine was equally repelled by Pelagius' teaching that the best way to encourage a person's mind to goodness was by teaching that it is possible to achieve anything if only you really want to. The fight for Christian truth between them and their followers went on for years.

If you have ever wondered why it is Christians seem to be so pre-occupied with sin, here is at least part of the answer. At the heart of our identity is a recognition both that we have a relationship with God and that this relationship is not as it should be. So when Pelagius speaks about being good, he claims that everything is possible:

> A person can pray to God worthily, pouring forth requests from a good conscience, and can say, 'You know, Lord, how holy, how innocent, how pure from all deceit and harm and wrongdoing are these hands which I reach out to you; how righteous, and untainted, and free of lies are the lips with which I cry to you so that you have mercy upon me.' Such a person deserves to be heard, and can obtain what they ask for.

I suspect that Augustine's response to that would be to point to the parable of the Pharisee and the tax-collector (Luke 18:9–14). One approach may be more logical and positive; the other is more honest and realistic. It can all be summed up in Pelagius' teaching, which is so clear and straightforward, and so wrong: 'Righteousness is simply not sinning. And not sinning is keeping the law.'

In his early years as a Christian, Augustine had thought that it was possible for us to 'deserve' the blessings of faith and the working of the Holy Spirit in our lives, provided that when God called us, we accepted that duty to follow the one calling, as a free choice. He had also believed then, and taught, that so long as we stayed in that relationship of faith, we would 'deserve' eternal life. In simple terms, this makes faith an action or decision of the believer, on the basis of which God decides to 'elect' that person.

But it wasn't long before Augustine had reflected more deeply on Paul's writings and worked out the weakness of this viewpoint. Then he began to teach instead that our 'election' (Romans 9:11; 11:28) is through God's grace, which goes before any and all merits we may lay claim to – including the merits of faith. He was well aware how difficult this belief would appear, and admitted as much when writing to his friend Simplicianus:

> In solving this question I strove to defend the free judgement of the human will, but the grace of God prevailed! In many places Paul bears witness (putting the grace of faith ahead of works) not to do away with works, but to show that works do not precede grace, but rather follow after it. This is undoubtedly so that no one judges themselves to have 'achieved' grace because they have done good works, but instead judges that they cannot do good works unless they have achieved grace through faith.

What we would call 'nature and nurture', two different influences at work in every human being in their moral choices and their faith, combine to create a force that drives us towards sin – and that combined force is so powerful that only divine grace can overcome it:

> We are born into this life in original sin [this is his way of thinking of the inevitability of our sinning], we add to it by committing habitual sins during the course of our life. These two factors, which we can call 'nature and habit', when joined

together, effect a virtually indestructible appetite for desiring, which Paul calls 'sin.' He says it is present in his own body, that is to say it exercises control and lordship over him.

It was not Augustine's style, not in his nature, to be rude or unkind to people he disagreed with. But he comes pretty close in his arguments with Pelagius, I think because he was so worried by the danger of people being encouraged to a wrong understanding of God's grace:

> I contended fiercely with the enemies of God's grace by which the unrighteous is justified. I obtained a certain book by Pelagius, in which, with his most powerful arguments, he defends human nature against God's grace (which justifies the unrighteous and in virtue of which we are Christians). I responded to him, defending grace as being not contrary to nature, and stating that it was the means by which our human nature is liberated and governed.

Augustine finally loses his patience with the idea that we can achieve a right relationship with God through our own efforts: this is because it becomes clear to him that Pelagius' way of being Christian makes even baptism itself a pointless exercise, with no meaning or value. We don't need to be washed for the cleansing of our sins if all we have to do is try a bit harder and behave a bit better! Unlike Pelagius, Augustine had learned the vital Christian lesson that perfectionism is not only unachievable but also undesirable – because it encourages us to think that we can achieve what God gives us as a free and unearned gift. Here, finally, is Augustine the teacher telling us what he does when he finds a fellow-Christian is in error. He does not rant or condemn, but has learned to be patient and positive, because God in Christ has shown him that this is the way that wins people to faith and repentance:

> Nowadays, when I hear one of my Christian brothers who is ignorant about some subject or other, and believes one thing rather than another, I regard him with patience while he

expresses his view. Nor do I see him as having a problem if he happens to be ignorant about how God's creation *is* or how it *appears*, provided that he has no beliefs which are unworthy of you, O Lord, creator of all.

Bible passage for reflection

There is one body and one Spirit, just as you were called to the one hope of your calling, one Lord, one faith, one baptism, one God and Father of all, who is above all and through all and in all. But each of us was given grace according to the measure of Christ's gift… The gifts he gave were that some would be apostles, some prophets, some evangelists, some pastors and teachers, to equip the saints for the work of ministry, for building up the body of Christ, until all of us come to the unity of the faith and of the knowledge of the Son of God, to maturity, to the measure of the full stature of Christ. We must no longer be children, tossed to and fro and blown about by every wind of doctrine, by people's trickery, by their craftiness in deceitful scheming. But speaking the truth in love, we must grow up in every way into him who is the head, into Christ, from whom the whole body, joined and knit together by every ligament with which it is equipped, as each part is working properly, promotes the body's growth in building itself up in love.

EPHESIANS 4:4–7, 11–16

What Paul gives us here is, first, a vision of true Christian unity and, second, a blueprint for managing disagreements, based on his understanding of God's grace. We do not all have the same role within the community of faith, for we are all different and our gifts and talents are different. But our purpose is the same for all – to build up the body of Christ. In the end, knowledge of Jesus Christ, and conformity to Jesus Christ are inseparable from Christian unity. As long as we are divided from one another, we are failing in our mission of being that body of Christ here on earth. And the threats to our faith and calling are real: threats from hostility, cynicism, indifference, threats from those who see the faith of others as a path to power for themselves. Our calling, in the end, is – in that beautiful phrase of Paul's – to *speak the truth in love*. And let God take care of everything else.

Questions

1 Does it matter that Christians don't always agree with one another?
2 What is the best way to deal with disagreements – to choose one side and reject the other, or to live with the tension?
3 Donatism and Pelagianism were the 'baddies' of their day. Who, for today's Christians, are the real 'baddies' (in other words, where are the real threats to authentic Christian faith coming from)?
4 Is grace an easy thing for Christians to understand? Can we explain it to non-Christians?

Prayer

Lord God, we are not very good at showing your love in our lives.
So much stuff gets in the way:
vanity and pride; our own selfishness;
the mistakes we make about what's really your will,
and what's really only ours.
Help us always to speak the truth in love,
to guard our tongues from unkind and impatient words,
and to remember Jesus' words from the cross,
'Father forgive them, for they know not what they do.' Amen

4

After conversion: living as a Christian

We have seen how important it was to Augustine to write about how he became a Christian. He records his conversion in detail, reflecting years afterwards on the meaning of it, just as Paul did in the New Testament. For anyone who has had a similar experience, it can be tempting to put too much emphasis on that 'conversion moment'. Its impact is so intense, so life-changing, that it comes to dominate the thinking of the person concerned. Understandable though this is, it also carries with it a risk: the risk of overemphasising the *moment* of conversion at the expense of the *process* of conversion. For conversion is always both these things. First, it is a moment in time; then it is a lifelong process in the mind and heart of the believer.

Augustine was aware of this risk. He knew that how we *live* as Christians is at least as important as how we *become* Christians. And so he tackled this question in his usual way, by writing a book. Even among all the big battles he had to fight for Christian truth, he managed to make time for a small guidebook for Christians, on the basics of living the life of faith.

As we have discovered, Augustine wrote a lot of books. Some were dense and challenging, like his 15 books on the Trinity or his 22 books about the city of God. But he didn't just cater for professional scholars, clergy like himself. He also thought about the needs of ordinary people trying to live their Christian lives as best they could:

When someone asked me for some sort of short work that he could have constantly to hand, I wrote a book called *On Faith, Hope and Love*. I think I have made a decent effort at encapsulating how God should be worshipped, which holy scripture defines as the true wisdom of humankind.

We know that he thought a lot about those three Christian virtues, not just from this little book but from things he says in other contexts:

Faith gives way to the sight of visible reality, and hope will make way for attainment of fulfilment. But love will actually increase when faith and hope have passed away.

This little book does tackle faith, hope and love, but within a few pages it also touches on other vital matters:

- the origin and nature of evil (that favourite preoccupation of Augustine himself);
- the place of reason in the life of faith;
- grace and original sin;
- the person and work of Christ;
- the resurrection;
- the Apostles' Creed and the Lord's Prayer.

But it is much more than a list of instructions or set of arguments. As always, Augustine isn't just interested in people doing the right thing; he cares about us doing the right thing *for the right reasons*. That's why, before everything else, he starts with worship, pointing out that worship and wisdom go together, and taking Job as his example:

'The fear of the Lord, that is wisdom; and to depart from evil is understanding' [Job 28:28]. God should be worshipped through faith, hope and love.

That general principle swiftly moves into touching on something as relevant today as it was all those centuries ago, as he poses the question, 'To what extent should reason support faith?' In a way, he has already answered his own question by writing his book – and you have agreed with him, by buying and reading this book! The Christian life is faith seeking understanding, and always has been. There is nothing to be afraid of in asking hard questions, because we can find in the Bible so many examples of people doing just that, and God affirms them in their questioning.

Augustine doesn't try to start from an 'objective' viewpoint. Just as well, since where God is concerned, there is no such thing. Whether we start our search for truth from the angle of believing or begin by not believing, we still have to start somewhere. For Augustine, every argument, every fact, every truth has one foundation: Christ. Augustine chooses to focus on faith, hope and love, in his little guidebook to Christian basics, because he sees them as the content and the point of true religion. We can gain knowledge of these three things that last forever by both our senses and our reason (our mind or intellect).

In addition to these two God-given ways of making sense of the world (physical and mental), says Augustine, we have the Bible, which gives us an independent viewpoint, outside our individual experience. We can trust the Bible, because it has been tested and found to deserve that trust. The experience of previous Christians is the foundation on which we build our own faith. Our aim should be something more than getting through the days, ticking the boxes – 'Been to church? Tick. Read my Bible? Tick.' The Christian life is a high calling, and the aim of our faith is to bring us to a clear and true vision of God, who is beauty itself. Augustine doesn't refer to 2 Peter, but his vision of the ultimate goal of a Christian life is very similar to the one spelled out in that letter:

> [God] has given us, through these things, his precious and very great promises, so that through them you may escape from

the corruption that is in the world because of lust, and may become participants in the divine nature.
2 PETER 1:4

Certainly for Augustine, the greatest happiness we are capable of consists precisely in this. But he knows that we are by no means ready to go straight from confessing our faith to reaching such a vision of God. First, we have a lot of work to do, to build on the basic foundations of faith, hope and love. Augustine is too wise, and too realistic, to set the bar so high. That would set most Christians up for failure and perhaps disillusionment. Instead, he sets it low, so that our first efforts to strive for God do not end in failure and giving up:

You have the Creed and the Lord's Prayer. What is shorter to listen to or read? What is more easily memorised?

He would have taken it for granted that people would learn such prayers by heart. Few people in his day could read, because education was so expensive. It is sad to think that we perhaps take this ability so much for granted, when it opens to us all the treasures of knowledge (Colossians 2:3). The Apostles' Creed was a prayer of faith from the earliest days of Christianity (see page 64 for the full text). Before the writings of the New Testament came together, people didn't become Christians by reading their Bible, because there was (as yet) no Bible. They learned it through mission, through being told the story of Jesus and what God had done through him, and then by deciding to be baptised into the community of believers. They learned it through worshipping together. The Apostles' Creed was the prayer they used to affirm their faith at the time of their baptism. So it is not as old as the Lord's Prayer, but it is still fundamental as a statement of Christian belief. In *Confessions*, Augustine refers to the creed as part of how converts affirm their new Christian identity:

New Christians usually repeat the Apostles' Creed from memory according to a set form of words, in a prominent place and in the sight of the Christian community.

Augustine thinks of the creed as a way of declaring or witnessing to our faith, which may seem like milk for babies in human terms, but in spiritual terms, he says, it is food for the strong and strengthens those who are faithful with hope and holy love. But as always, he is not interested in mindless repetition of holy words as a way of earning credit with God. What matters to him is the inner motivation that prompts us to act as we do:

> When we ask whether a person is good, we are not asking what they believe or what they hope for but what they *love*.

It is as if he has taken the words of Jesus in the sermon on the mount and made them the measure of every Christian life and every Christian action:

> Store up for yourselves treasures in heaven, where neither moth nor rust consumes and where thieves do not break in and steal. For where your treasure is, there your heart will be also.
> MATTHEW 6:20–21

Nor does he take it for granted that everyone understands what we mean when we talk about faith, hope and love. Augustine does not forget to explain what faith, hope and love actually *are*. I found it helpful to read his simple insight that faith can refer to something past, present or future, and which can be good or bad (he is thinking of passages like James 2:19, where even the demons believe in – or 'have faith in' – God, and they tremble). Hope, on the other hand, must refer to something in the future, something that is good (as in Romans 8:24–25). But all three, he insists, are bound up together:

> There is no love without hope, and no hope without love: and neither without faith.

All this is positive guidance. It sets out what we are to strive for. But Augustine does not let his reader do only the easy bits; he wants us to think about the hard question of evil, too. As I said before, this question bothered him all his life, and he never stopped searching for answers, for understanding. In *Confessions*, he describes how he used to worry about why evil exists and what it is:

> I began to seek feverishly for the origin of evil. How great were the torments of my heart, as it went into labour, O my God, and the cries of pain! And your ears were there to hear, though I did not know it. Though I searched valiantly in silence, the silent sufferings of my soul were loud cries for your mercy.

Perhaps most Christians would not worry as much as Augustine does about this exact question. But many of us are familiar with how one difficult question about our faith can become a constant worry, a nagging sore. Although he found no completely satisfactory answer to the question of evil, Augustine did find something just as valuable and important: peace of mind. He saw that once we are clear about the basic point that God is good, and made us good, that is enough reassurance to carry us through the difficult questions we don't fully understand. Baptism is the way for Christians to put the sinful aspects of their nature into God's hands; not because it protects us from sin by making us perfect, but because it puts us in a place where we can start again, clean, knowing that what we do wrong must be faced through repentance and confession:

> Each person is reborn in baptism in such a way that whatever sin is within them when they are born, it is entirely repaid. Sins committed afterwards by wrongdoing can also be healed by penitence, as we see happening even after baptism.

Jesus, Augustine thinks, was baptised not to wash away sin, because he was without sin. Instead, it was something he accepted voluntarily, out of 'merciful goodwill' – in the same way that he accepted death on the cross even though he did not 'need' to experience death at all. God gave all humanity a free choice about good and evil; and choosing baptism is a way of showing that we are ready to choose the good.

When he talks about infancy and childhood in *Confessions*, Augustine describes the behaviour of small babies with a psychological insight that is striking. He does not sentimentalise, although he has a deeply loving nature as a father. He 'reads' the action of a little one without prejudice and sees the child's eagerness and greed to feed at the breast, and get more than its sibling who is also being nursed, as a primal appetite, a *drive*, if you like, to secure sustenance at any cost, competing with others if necessary. It is completely natural when viewed from a biological perspective – and deeply selfish viewed from an ethical perspective. His description of this simple insight is refreshing in its honesty.

Augustine had a loving nature, but he did not believe in deceiving himself out of kindness or sentiment. 'Honesty is the best policy' could have been his watchword. In the book of Job, Augustine found words that spoke to him on this subject with great force: 'A mortal, born of woman, [is] few of days and full of trouble' (Job 14:1). Yet even our impatience for good things to come to us; our restless desire for possession, control, resources; our hunger for attention and affirmation: all these things become God's means of grace, a way for God to make us aware of how much we need him. It is a wonderfully positive 'take' on some dark words of warning.

It is beyond the scope of this book to go into detail about all the subjects Augustine manages to cover – in fact, I find myself full of admiration at how much he packs into such a small book – but one thing we do need to look into with his help is the matter of our salvation. Augustine points out that the clue to Christ's nature is in the very name Jesus, which means the one who 'saves/heals' (it is the same word in Greek and Latin, so we have to keep both ideas in mind). Christ must be different from us (i.e. divine) or he himself would need to be saved as we need to be saved; and Christ must also be somehow the same as us (i.e. human), because what is not part of his nature cannot be one with him and so could not be saved. He is concerned to offer us reassurance that the divine and human natures in Christ are not just a theoretical teaching we have to sign up to, but a living reality for us to feel in our hearts as well as accept in our minds. The way to take this truth to ourselves, he tells us, is through the church, the community of faithful Christians. And this is also the way that we share the truth with other people.

When he explores this difficult subject of what it means to be a human being, made in God's image and likeness yet somehow also at a distance from him, Augustine makes a brief comment that, if you were reading his handbook in a hurry, might escape your attention completely. I am very glad that I did notice it, and I have thought a lot about it since. The comment is short and sweet: 'Christ did not die for the angels.'

Augustine had no doubt that angels were real, that they were (as their name in Greek indicates) messengers sent by God, as the Bible repeatedly tells us. And we also know from the Bible that they are so blessed and holy that they abide in God's presence (Isaiah 6:1–3). But Christ did not die for the angels. He died for *us*.

I remember years ago reading the words of an old-fashioned children's hymn, 'There's a friend for little children above the bright blue sky'. The hymn was written by Albert Midlane in 1859. Nowadays it sounds very dated, but one idea in it caught my eye and made me think, and it was wonderful to discover that Augustine had come to exactly the same realisation so many years before Midlane:

There's a song for little children, above the bright blue sky,
A song that will not weary, though sung continually;
A song which even angels can never, never sing:
They know not Christ as Saviour, but worship him as king.

It is a wonderful thing to know that Christ died for us. But even more wonderful to realise that *the fact of being saved* is a blessing in itself, a blessing that only those who have once lost their way can know. Like Augustine himself, it is those who have known sin and separation from God who are most grateful for being restored to his love and presence – like the lost sheep or the sick person in need of healing (Luke 15:4–7; Matthew 9:12–13).

While he reflects on these spiritual matters, Augustine doesn't forget to make suggestions about the more practical choices facing Christians in their daily lives. He knows that it is not good for us to look after our own needs and neglect those of other people, and he points to what Jesus says in Luke 11:41 ('Give for alms those things that are within; and see, everything will be clean for you') as being vital advice for Christians to follow, because what it commends to us is not theoretical but practical: a response that Augustine describes as 'constructive compassion'.

In order to live the Christian life properly, fully, we have to learn to join up our feelings of compassion with our duty to let go of wrongs done to us, so that whatever challenge we face in Christian living, we can meet it with the same response – love. That is why, Augustine says, the best prayer is the Lord's Prayer: it combines *forgiving* and *forgiven-ness*. And if we learn our duty well, we see our principles blend seamlessly with our way of life, because 'no kind of charitable action is greater than to forgive from the heart what another person has done against us'.

In the end, everything comes back to love; which is greater than anything else we can do to demonstrate our love for God. That is the clear message of 1 Corinthians 13, and also of Galatians 5:6: 'In Christ Jesus neither circumcision nor uncircumcision counts for anything; the only thing that counts is faith working through love.'

Every divine command, Augustine concludes, comes back to that same principle of love. The goal of every law of God is love, because love is the fulfilling of the law (Romans 13:10). Ultimately all this is true because God himself *is* love (1 John 4.16). When we grow in love, our selfish human appetites (for food, money, pleasure, praise, status) all diminish. It really is possible to grow in holiness if we follow the way of the cross and live by the message of the gospel.

There is a famous saying of Augustine's we haven't yet met in this book, which seems both outrageous and somehow also so right when we hear it. A few years ago, I did a workshop with inmates serving life sentences at a high-security prison, and we spent time studying together and looking at what we could learn from Augustine. For me, one of the best things about doing this workshop was seeing how directly and simply Augustine spoke from centuries ago to those men. We looked first at the story of the theft of pears, which we have already considered (see page 18). That got the men into a powerful discussion about the roots of wrongdoing and the power of peer pressure. Then we went on to this famous saying, and it made an even stronger impact on them, perhaps because of its paradoxical nature and its deceptive simplicity:

You must accept one simple rule: love, and do what you want.

I didn't get a chance to talk in detail about why this appealed to the men so much, but I got the impression it wasn't because it made light of what they had done. It was – I think – because it looked behind the legal transgression and asked about the motivation behind the deed. That is not meant to lessen the wrongness of their offending, but it was a way of thinking about their lives that started with the person they wanted to be, the person they set out to be, and not the person the system they had transgressed against condemned them for being. I can't be sure that this was true of all of them to the same extent, of course. But I'm sure it was true to a large extent of some of them. And this man from history had taught them that principle of love:

If you correct, correct out of love; if you spare, spare out of love. Let the root of love be within you, for nothing but good can come from that root.

Augustine is not recommending a 'whatever' way of living your life. He truly believes, and means to teach, that correct understanding of the person and work of Christ are vital if faith, hope and love are to flourish in a person. Once again, motivation is everything. Our intention to love in all aspects of our lives must be the fruit of our love of God, and of his Son Jesus Christ. Right belief and behaviour matter, even though without love they are worthless (1 Corinthians 13:1–3).

Bible passage for reflection

I am writing these instructions to you so that, if I am delayed, you may know how one ought to behave in the household of God, which is the church of the living God, the pillar and bulwark of the truth. Without any doubt, the mystery of our religion is great:

He was revealed in flesh,
    vindicated in spirit,
    seen by angels,
proclaimed among Gentiles,
    believed in throughout the world,
    taken up in glory.

Now the Spirit expressly says that in later times some will renounce the faith by paying attention to deceitful spirits and teachings of demons, through the hypocrisy of liars whose consciences are seared with a hot iron. They forbid marriage and demand abstinence from foods, which God created to be received with thanksgiving by those who believe and know the truth. For everything created by God is good, and nothing is to be rejected, provided it is received with thanksgiving; for it is sanctified by God's word and by prayer.

If you put these instructions before the brothers and sisters, you will be a good servant of Christ Jesus, nourished on the words of the faith and of the sound teaching that you have followed.

1 TIMOTHY 3:14—4:6

This advice from Paul is all about how to live as a Christian community. What stands out about it, it in the light of what we've learned about Augustine in this chapter, is how behaviour and belief must go together. It really matters that we live our lives as Christian people ought to live, and it really matters that we believe what Christian people have to believe if we can have the right to call ourselves 'Christian' at all. The way is not easy. There are all too many ways to be tempted, distracted and led into sin. But we are to fix our eyes on Jesus, who is both pioneer and perfecter of our faith (Hebrews 12:2); with his example always before us, surely our feet will not stray far from the way.

Question

For this chapter, I don't have a set of questions for you to tackle, only one. But it's a big question! We have seen how Augustine summarised the most important things about Christianity into one small book, called *Faith, Hope and Love*. (Its other title is *Enchiridion*.) I have done my best to pick out here the elements of that book that are most helpful for Christians today. But some of the topics he covers in his book are by no means as central in our thinking now as they were in his day. Things have moved on, as they always do. For example, I don't think we are as bothered as he was about the problem of the origin of evil. I would say that the reasons for the existence of suffering are probably more important to today's Christians than the nature of evil.

Of course, I can't know what is going on inside the minds and hearts of fellow Christians, but when you spend a lot of time, as I do, talking to people about their spiritual life, you do start to get some impressions of where the key difficulties lie. In the same way, I don't believe most Christians today are as bothered about defining the person and work of Christ as they were back then. For us, those questions were asked and answered a thousand years ago. But to Augustine they are fresh and pressing. Similarly, I would be surprised if many of us today are worried about things like the causes of sin, the nature of angels and the meaning of the church. For me, the biggest gap in what Augustine has to say is that there is nothing about worship in his handbook. Perhaps he has taken that bit as a given, something that didn't need saying because everyone understood it; but I can't know that for certain.

So my one big question for this chapter is this:

● If you gave yourself the same job as Augustine – to write a short book (a maximum of 100 pages) setting out the key essentials of Christianity – what would you include? Think about teaching (what to believe as a Christian), ethics (how to live as a Christian), basic elements (prayers, words, even hymns); and any other things that you consider absolutely essential. What would your Christian Handbook contain, and why?

Prayer

Teach me, O Lord, the way of your laws,
and I shall keep it till the end;
but for that I need your help and guidance,
and a spirit of self-discipline,
not to fail when kindness costs,
and when duty is dull and difficult.
Make me always mindful that I am a sinner in need of forgiveness,
and that I owe a debt of forgiveness
to my fellow human beings. Amen

The Apostle's Creed

I believe in God, the Father almighty, creator of heaven and earth; and in Jesus Christ his only Son, our Lord, who was conceived from the Holy Spirit, and born of the virgin Mary, who suffered under Pontius Pilate, and who was crucified, dead and buried. He went down into the depths of the earth. On the third day he arose from the dead, ascended to the heavens, and took his seat at the right hand of God the almighty Father. From there he will come to judge the living and the dead. I believe in the Holy Spirit, the holy, universal church, the communion of saints, the forgiveness of sins, the resurrection of the body, and eternal life.

5

From learner to teacher

So far, we have seen Augustine as a student of the Bible. Later in his life, however, he was also a preacher and teacher, one of the most famous in the world. People wanted him to visit them, preach to them, teach them:

> We walk by faith, not sight: faith will totter if the authority of the holy Bible wavers. Those who fall from faith must also fall from love; for they cannot love what they do not believe in.

The Bible was not something he accepted for his own personal interest and pleasure, not even for his own spiritual improvement or growth. It was a book that spoke to him, and it gave him a message, loud and clear, that he must make it known to others. He describes this feeling of a need to share the message when he talks about his love for the Psalms in his *Confessions*:

> What cries I uttered to you, my God, while I was reading the psalms of David, those songs full of faith, sounds of devotion that exclude a spirit of pride! I was clumsy about my love for you, but sincere. What cries I uttered to you in those psalms! How they set me ablaze for you, and made me burn to chant them to the whole world – if I could – to challenge the human race's pride! They are sung all over the world, and 'there is no one who can hide from your heat' [Psalm 19:6].

These are not the words of a man who treats his Bible merely as an academic text. When we read of his love and inspiration, it is easy to see why his symbol in Christian art is a heart pierced by a flaming arrow. These are words of love – love for God and love for his holy word. The words of the psalms set him ablaze, he tells us. Again, this is not just to inspire him in himself but also to awaken his calling to preach them to others, to offer them as a gift and a challenge to the whole human race. When we read this, it is easy to understand how he kept people listening when he preached, sometimes for hours at a time. His love for God, like his love for the Bible, is infectious. It makes me think of the old saying, 'Christianity is caught, not taught.'

When he first became a priest, Augustine wanted to take time to study the Bible, because he knew that his knowledge was inadequate to sustain a lifetime of preaching and teaching. It was always going to be difficult to make that time, given all the other demands for his attention, but he managed it. And just as well, given that in those days sermons could go on for hours and were delivered without any notes. His training as a public speaker came in handy here, as did his equally well-trained memory. But these two things alone would not have been enough. The Bible had to matter to him, his love for the holy word had to shine in his preaching and set others aglow. And it did. To those who listened, all the hard work and study and prayer were invisible. They saw and heard the end result, preaching that was powerful, persuasive, inspiring. But to those who also had a calling themselves to preach the gospel, there was another element in Augustine's Bible teaching that was invaluable – he showed them how to be better preachers themselves. Although he did this principally through the example of his own preaching, he also did what came naturally to him, and wrote a book about it. It was called *How to Teach Christianity* (or *On Christian Teaching*), a sort of manual for ministers that was mainly about how to understand the Bible and communicate its message to Christians and non-Christians alike.

Augustine was a preacher for many decades. He preached over 8,000 sermons, some of which were three hours long. We still have hundreds of them available to read today, and more are still being discovered. He understood the importance of starting 'where people are' (as we would say today), not talking down to them or mystifying them with spiritual jargon. And he never behaved as though he was dispensing divine wisdom from some higher level; he reminded his hearers, 'We are all students here, both you and me.' Though his ministry as a preacher brought him fame and admiration, he never let it go to his head:

> The preachers of your word pass from this life to another life. But still your scripture reaches out covering all your peoples, to the end of the age. Both heaven and earth will pass away, but your words will not pass away.

He saw himself as 'only' the medium, not the message. His task was to preach Christ, not himself. And it was no good, he knew, preaching to people in a way that went over their heads:

> How could a teacher be ready to be spent for their souls while not accepting the need to adapt to fit their ears? This was why Christ became a little child in the midst of us, like a nurse tending her own children.

Augustine knew that once he had done his best to preach God's word, the rest was out of his hands; and yet his love for his people meant that he always worried about whether he was getting the gospel message across in the most effective way:

> What do I want? What do I long for? Why am I speaking? Why am I alive? – if not with this purpose, that we may live together with Christ. If I have proclaimed the word to you, and you have not listened to me, my own soul may be free of responsibility for you. But even so, I do not want to be saved without you.

He understood that people often reach out to God and start to search for him from quite mixed and complicated motives, not all of them positive. Fear often plays a part in their yearning for God. In fact, Augustine went so far as to say that it was rare for anyone to want to become a Christian who had not been struck by some sort of fear of God. But instead of working on that fear, to increase it and terrify the person into conversion, Augustine would always encourage them to think of things differently – to remember instead how greatly God cares for our well-being. To put the emphasis on love instead of fear is characteristic of the man. It had been his own experience – to start searching from fear, and stop when he discovered divine love – and that was what he wanted for other people, as well as for himself.

When students at my college in Cambridge decide to profess Christian faith, I encourage them to make a rule of life. This is an ancient practice, a way of setting boundaries so that we know when we are falling short or becoming spiritually lazy. Augustine tackles this matter too, as a warning that we always run the risk, when we fix rules and boundaries, of making them the highest level we aspire to, instead of the lowest level below which we will not go. Every time we set a spiritual target for ourselves (such as how often to say our prayers, read the Bible or go to church), it is possible we will slip into the mindset of 'Right, job done, box ticked, God served, now I can get on with life.' This is not a good idea, so we need to take care:

> The Lord had said to someone, 'Offer to God a sacrifice of praise,' so the man considered within himself and declared, 'I will get up every day, go to church, sing one of the morning hymns, another at evening, a third or fourth in my own home; daily I offer the sacrifice of praise, and make an offering to my God.' That is a good thing for anyone to decide and do; but be careful not to be careless because you do this – perhaps your tongue is blessing God while your way of life reviles him.

There is a serious warning in those words, and he is right to urge his listeners not to fall into the habit of thinking that prayers are enough without a reform of our way of life. He could preach that message with integrity, because he had *done* it. He had tried the words-only approach, and had to reject it in favour of the old truism 'Actions speak louder than words.' He had allowed other people, through his honest writings, to see that process at work in him, so that they could draw lessons from it for their own lives. That took real courage and humility for a man susceptible to pride. For a former professor of public speaking, this is quite an admission:

> When you talk to people about how they should behave, it is pointless to persuade them that what you say is true – and the style of your speaking is pointless too – unless they learn it *in such a way that they put it into action*.

Occasionally Augustine lets us see the private man, the individual Christian, who is torn by the conflict between his public role and his private Christian self. The following words, in which Augustine refers to the time when he was a bishop – and so the 'public face' of the church in the place where he lived – will resonate with anyone whose role in life demands that they sometimes have to cloak their private feelings for the sake of others' immediate needs (which is pretty much everyone):

> Sometimes my heart is besieged by some temptation or trouble, and at that moment someone says to me: Come and talk to so-and-so, he wants to become a Christian. But they speak without knowing what is consuming me deep within. If it is inappropriate to show my feelings to them, I am still reluctant to do as they ask.

He knows he has gifts that can help others, perhaps when they have lost their way, as he once had; perhaps when they are desperate to join the ranks of Christians, but some obstacle is in their way. He can see their problem, and he can see a way to help them out of it – so how could he *not* help, given their great need? He has a calling to help people start their journey into faith, and nothing is going to distract him from it. He shows us this in a passage from *Confessions* that I love because of the way he imagines new Christians as baby birds, needing to be brooded and protected in the nest until they are ready to fly:

Some people think of God as some kind of colossal authority figure. Such worldly people are still in their infancy, while the weak understanding is nestled in the simplest kind of language as if still being brooded by their mother. But their faith is being built up in a healthy way, to help them grasp and hold firm the fact that God has made all the natural phenomena, in their wondrous variety, which their sense-perceptions see all around them. If any of them were to scorn the words of scripture as too humble, and to lean forward out of their nurturing nest in all the weakness of their pride – alas! – poor creatures, they will fall. Lord God, have mercy, do not let those passing on their way trample your chicks when they are still not ready to fly. Send your angel to restore them to the nest, to live there till they fledge.

As we have seen, Augustine thought of the Bible as a sure source of inspired truth, given to human beings by God. But that didn't mean Christians could or should give up asking difficult questions about it. He believed that Moses wrote the Pentateuch, for example, but he also wondered about what was in the mind of Moses when he wrote those books. Sometimes, he concluded, it is not possible to decide for certain what the author of a text meant; we have to live with the ambiguity and uncertainty. On one occasion Augustine gets cross with someone who is being too dogmatic by claiming that they have sure knowledge about what Moses meant in those books. Augustine's reaction is very understandable:

If someone says, 'Moses did not mean what you say, but what I say', then, O Life of the poor, O my God, in whose heart there is no disagreement, let a soothing rain drop down upon my heart so that I can bear such people patiently!

He wants, as we often do ourselves, to find the strength to put up with people who shout the most but know the least, and in his kindly but plain criticism of their attitudes we find a perceptive understanding of what is really driving such people:

> They speak like this not because they are godlike and have seen into the heart of your servant Moses, but because they are proud. They do not know Moses's view, but love their own instead (not because it is true but because it is theirs). Their presumption betrays arrogance, not knowledge. It is born of pride, not vision.

Not everyone who sets out to teach Christianity does so from the starting point of love and humility, which Augustine recommends, and it is evidently frustrating to him that those who let their ego get in the way of the message are undermining the faith of those they claim to teach. Teaching is a serious responsibility, not to be undertaken lightly:

> By rashly asserting a meaning the writer did not intend, an interpreter can often run into other matters that they cannot make fit with the rest of the argument. Thus they come to love their own arguments more than scripture and find it, rather than themselves, objectionable. If they let this evil worm its way in, it will be their downfall.

Some of what Augustine writes and thinks about the Bible is not really in keeping with today's way of reading; like everyone else in his time he is quick to detect hidden meanings in verses that are not easy to interpret. But everything that he says, whether simple or complicated, begins from the same point: that God has made himself known in these holy books, and that every verse has something positive to say to us. There is nothing in scripture that is worthless or lacking in meaning. When Augustine sets out to teach the teachers, the ministers whose job it was to proclaim the message to their congregations Sunday by Sunday, he starts with matters so basic that we perhaps think they don't even need saying at all. So, for example, he asks why we read the Bible, and he answers by saying that those who read it are looking to find the thoughts and will of the people who wrote it down, and through them the will of God, because the Bible writers spoke in accordance with that divine will. He wonders why the meaning is sometimes so difficult to penetrate, and again comes up with a positive, robust answer – that when we have to put effort into answering questions it leads to more rewarding answers. And he warns would-be interpreters of the Bible against being arrogant in presuming they have got the message completely:

> We must let our devotion make us gentle, and submit to scripture, both when we understand it as it criticises our faults, and when we fail to understand it because we think we know better.

This reminder to start with humility, not arrogance, is clearly important to him, as he finds various ways to express it and so to hammer home the point. First he insists:

> Each person must first find in the Bible that they are entangled in love of this world, i.e. earthly things, and separated from the great love of God and the great love of neighbour which the Bible calls us to. This will make them want to improve their own situation.

Soon after this he reinforces his point by saying how vital it is that we read with 'a mind intent on mercy' because this makes it possible for us to love even our enemies. It is a gentle, non-judgemental warning against judgementalism. Only then can we win the prize that the Bible holds out to us, of wisdom and a mind at peace with itself and God.

Augustine starts with the most basic question of all, a question so basic that for many of my years as a Christian it never occurred to me to ask it: which books belong in the Bible and so have authority over Christians? Perhaps we don't think to ask this question because we are used to thinking of the Bible as a single book. We buy it as one volume with many chapters. But in Augustine's day, books were not like our books. They were hand-written paper rolls, and one roll was long enough for one Bible book. So not every Christian community would have all the books we think of as essential for knowing 'the Bible'. Hence the question of which ones had authority was very important back then, even though it seems obvious to us now.

He also explains another simple thing that we probably take for granted, so is well worth bearing in mind: the Bible gives us two sorts of information. The first is guidance for how to live: we would call this ethics or morals – what kind of behaviour, what way of life, is acceptable to God and what is forbidden for his faithful people. The second concerns our understanding of who, and what, God is and what we can know and say about him (what is called theology, or talk about God). God has woven these two materials together within the books of the Bible, so we must weave them together in our lives. You can't be a Christian *only* by living a moral life; nor can you be a Christian *only* by believing and saying the right things about God. It has to be both. Or at least we have to *try* to make it both.

There is also the matter of language to be tackled. Again, plenty of today's Christians never give this a thought. Their Bible is in English and that's that. Augustine didn't get off so lightly. He read the Bible in Latin, because that was his native language. But he knew that it was originally written in Hebrew and Greek, and he knew nothing of one language and not much of the other. But he didn't take the easy step of saying that the original languages didn't matter; he knew they did. What he did say is that we Christians need people who have studied the Bible languages, so that we can make sure our translations are accurate and can explain words and ideas we don't understand ourselves. Knowledge of languages is a way to guard against our misinterpreting things. But we don't all have to be experts; we simply need to listen to those who have studied and acquired this kind of knowledge and take their wisdom into account.

It is important to remember here that one of the reasons for the incredible power and appeal of the Christian message down the centuries is that it has not been fossilised in the original ancient languages. We don't have to study Hebrew and Greek to be able to call ourselves proper Christians. The Bible is every bit as much the inspired word of God in English, Welsh, Latin or any other language as it is in its original languages. God speaks to us through the word, the message, contained in the words. He is not trapped inside the original language versions like a genie in a lamp!

One thing Augustine could never bring himself to say is that the Bible was wrong; he simply didn't believe that such a thing was possible. Where a text is confusing, as sometimes happens because it isn't clear what the original word was, or what it meant, there must be another way to make sense of the passage. So, when he reads Isaiah 7:9, for example, he finds there are two versions of the verse to choose from: 'If you do not believe, you will not understand' and 'If you do not believe, you will not stand fast.' He concludes that sometimes both versions yield a 'worthy' meaning. It simply means that the Bible is even richer in meaning than we originally thought.

Sometimes this way of looking for meaning carries him beyond what is merely historical. It is important for us to see him making use of the imagination when reading the Bible, because our reading should never be confined to a sterile search for facts and rules. As long as we are careful to remember what is clearly there in the text, it is worthwhile to let our imagination work on it, because it will sometimes carry us into surprising and wonderful places.

A good example of this is what Augustine finds in Ephesians 3:18–19. It is a passage we would expect to appeal to him because of its teaching on love, but he finds more in it than I had ever done before I read these words of his. Here is the passage:

> I pray that you may have the power to comprehend, with all the saints, what is the breadth and length and height and depth, and to know the love of Christ that surpasses knowledge, so that you may be filled with all the fullness of God.

And here is Augustine's reflection:

> Ephesians 3:18 stands for the Lord's cross – 'breadth' is the crossbeam; 'length' is the beam from the ground to the centre of the cross; 'height' is the beam from the centre to the top; 'depth' is the hidden part set in the ground. On this sign of the cross every Christian act is inscribed: behaving well 'in Christ'; cleaving to him for ever; hoping for heavenly things; honouring the sacraments. Cleansed by such action we shall have the strength to understand the love of Christ which surpasses all.

Anyone who sets out to read their Bible has to begin at the beginning, with the basics: find a reliable translation; use plain passages where the teaching is clear to help you make sense of the more difficult passages; don't take things literally that are not meant to be taken literally, because, Augustine reminds us of Paul's maxim, 'the letter kills, but the Spirit gives life' (2 Corinthians 3:6). Once we have true understanding, there is no risk that we will create idols for ourselves and worship the created things (like the world, or even the Bible) rather than the creator. This leads to spiritual freedom.

I would be surprised if many people today know their Bible better than Augustine knew his. He was an eager reader all his life, but nothing was remotely as important to him as this book, which still matters so much to us. But even though he knew it intimately, in incredible detail, he still had the insight to boil it down to a pure essence:

> What does scripture do? It commends nothing but love, condemns nothing but greed. It asserts the universal faith in matters past, present and future: it tells the story of the past, it foreshadows the future and it reveals the present. And it does all these things to feed and strengthen love and overcome selfish desire.

He understood that not every verse could possibly apply equally to everyone, so it was important not to lose sight of the wood (the overall message) for the trees (individual points of teaching).

People, he argued, speak more or less wisely in proportion to their proficiency in holy scripture – not in terms of argument or memorising, but by means of true understanding and a faithful search for meaning. The message was a universal one:

> There is virtually no page of the holy books in which the principle that 'God resists the proud but gives grace to the humble' (James 4:6) does not resound.

But it needed to be well taught if people were to take that message to heart. He doesn't think much of teachers who let showing off their knowledge get in the way of real communication:

> What is the use of paying no attention to the audience's understanding? There is absolutely no point in speaking if the people to whom we are speaking, supposedly to help them understand, do not have a clue what we are talking about!

And just in case the preachers he is trying to guide get carried away with their own skill, Augustine has a kindly but firm reminder for them:

> This is what eloquence means in teaching: not being able to make something nasty seem appealing, or to talk people into taking action where they were originally reluctant. No. It is to make clear what was hidden. If this is done in an unattractive way, it leads to a poor yield, and only the most determined students (those who want to learn even though the method of teaching is unpolished) will get anything out of it.

They should never forget that anyone who teaches must first be open to learning from God. Even more importantly, they must be aware that those who listen to them will be listening not only to what they say, but also what they do not say. In other words, their way of life, whether or not they realise it, will be the yardstick by which their words and persuasions are measured. So teachers of

Christian faith must 'let their way of life speak eloquently in support of their words'.

When it comes to reading the Bible, the same principle is at work as in every other aspect of Christian living, Augustine argues. Everything must be about love. On the basis of his own experience, he is convinced that people need to be taught how to love, or, to be more precise, they need to be taught how to love themselves in a way that does them good rather than harm. The kind of love he means is not about letting ourselves off the hook or indulging ourselves. We are called to love all God's children equally. But we are finite, and our emotional resources are finite. So because we can't be of service to everyone, we must focus our efforts on the people who 'seeming chance' (Augustine's phrase) has set most closely beside us in place, time and circumstances.

Again, we cannot love everyone in the same kind of way, even though we share Christian faith. Some people we love because we help them, some because they help us; some because we need their support, some because they need ours. And there are always some we have nothing to offer, and who have nothing in common with us either. But we should still want every single one of them to love God with us whether or not we feel close to them as people.

In this chapter I have let Augustine speak very much in his own words, because they are so straightforward and compelling, as fresh and relevant as when they were first written. Let me end this chapter with two final insights into the role of a teacher:

> Students of holy scripture who are trained in this way, when they begin to analyse it in detail must meditate constantly on the apostolic saying, 'Knowledge puffs up, but love builds up.'

> Those who teach the faith must begin with prayer: by praying for themselves and for those they are about to address. They must be people of prayer before they are people of words.

Bible passage for reflection

How beautiful upon the mountains
    are the feet of the messenger who announces peace,
who brings good news,
    who announces salvation,
    who says to Zion, 'Your God reigns.'
Listen! Your sentinels lift up their voices,
    together they sing for joy;
for in plain sight they see
    the return of the Lord to Zion.
Break forth together into singing,
    you ruins of Jerusalem;
for the Lord has comforted his people,
    he has redeemed Jerusalem.
The Lord has bared his holy arm
    before the eyes of all the nations;
and all the ends of the earth shall see
    the salvation of our God.

Depart, depart, go out from there!
    Touch no unclean thing;
go out from the midst of it, purify yourselves,
    you who carry the vessels of the Lord.
For you shall not go out in haste,
    and you shall not go in flight;
for the Lord will go before you,
    and the God of Israel will be your rearguard.

ISAIAH 52:7–12

These are words of the prophet Isaiah, who Augustine found so hard to read back when he was first getting to know the Bible. They are famous words, words that can be understood in many ways, but in one way they speak to everyone who has taken the Christian gospel to heart – how beautiful, indeed, is the message of peace from God, and that makes beautiful the one who brings it to us. As a teacher, like all teachers (including the ones who made his childhood miserable), Augustine had real power. He chose to use that power for good, to encourage people in their faith, to build them up, not to break them down. When God's message is truly proclaimed, it will be heard and people will respond, because the truth shines like a light in the darkness, and the darkness cannot overcome it (John 1:5).

Questions

1 Augustine says, in a handbook for preachers, that it is characteristic of good minds 'to love the truth in words, not the words themselves'. Do you agree?
2 In your Bible, do you think that the precise wording is crucial, or is it the 'gist' that counts most?
3 Who is the Christian teacher or preacher who has influenced you most, and why?
4 Is it true that love is the only motivation that matters?

Prayer

Lord God, open my mind to your Truth, revealed in the Bible;
open my heart, that I may drink in that Truth
and make it a part of who I am;
open my eyes to see the presence of the Truth in other people,
and to love all your children, for your name's sake. Amen

6

Augustine learns to pray with others

Being a Christian is not something any of us can do entirely on our own. Christianity is not a self-help movement for individuals; it is a shared faith. We need one another to flourish and to grow. Even so, many of our struggles with faith, and about God, happen in isolation. This is partly in the nature of faith itself – it is when we are on our own, no one to pretend to, no one to hide from, that the questions of life and meaning (and sometimes the doubts and fears) come thick and fast. We spend so much of our lives filling up our time with busy nothings, to stop ourselves from thinking and, in fact, to block out the voice of God that is always calling us by name.

Another factor is that it can be difficult to share our weaknesses and fears with other Christians. We may be afraid that they will judge us or be disappointed in us, if we admit that sometimes we have doubts or struggle with temptations and distractions. Augustine was just like us in this respect too. He wanted to be part of that body of believers we call the church, but he also had his individual relationship with God to work on and to work out. Both these elements in our faith go on at the same time; one is sometimes dominant over the other, but both are always necessary.

So far, we have seen Augustine coming to terms with his need for God – letting go of his old self, studying his Bible, stepping out into the unknown to struggle for the truth as he believed it. Now it is time to see how he learned what to do next – how to accept his need for the community of believers and the support of fellow Christians, and how to pray with others in times of worship. In the next chapter, we will look at how he finally learned to pray by himself.

As we have seen, Augustine was the first person in European history to describe in detail, and with psychological insight, the human person as a unique individual. But he never lost sight of the fact that as human beings we are part of a whole, whether we call it the human species, the human race or the human family. We all have to learn how to live as part of a group, indeed, as part of many groups in the course of a lifetime. It is a process that begins in the family, develops through our education at school and finally spreads out into our working lives and social relationships. It can be difficult, but it is also liberating to realise that life is not just about us!

When Augustine tries to put this into words, he uses the language of a journey. This was part of how Christians have always understood themselves, right from the beginning. In Acts, the new faith is called 'the Way' – a path to be trodden, a direction to be taken (Acts 9:2; 19:9; 19:23). And ways, or roads, or paths, are only visible, and only last, because many people keep treading in the same place, wearing a visible, permanent mark on the land. One person walking alone leaves few traces, which soon vanish. But many people walking in the Way, for many centuries – they leave an indelible mark on history. You might expect Augustine, that clever professor of public speaking, that deep thinker, to consider himself above needing other people's help, even their company, on the Way. But he knows that he does need them, and admits it freely:

I make my confession to you, Lord, not only before you in secret delight but also in the hearing of those people who are believers. They are companions in my joy and share in the transience of our humanity. These are my fellow citizens and my fellow travellers, who go before me and who follow after, and who have a share in my life. These people are your servants and my brothers.

Christian faith is radical because it is a faith of equals. In Augustine's time there was no equality in terms of social status, education or anything else. There was a pecking order, and everyone knew their place. There was some degree of social mobility, but it was the rare exception not the norm. In contrast to these human standards, then and now, Christians all have the same status, the same value, because they are all God's beloved children. They are united by sharing in a common action, the action of Christian baptism:

> There is no one who does not need life, salvation (or 'health'), liberation, redemption, illumination. Baptism – in which we are buried with Christ – is part of all these things.

Christians are reborn when they are baptised, so, according to Augustine, they have two different ages – they have their biological age and they also have their Christian age. So, he tells us, because he and his son Adeodatus and his friend Alypius were all baptised together, as Christians they are all the same age.

Augustine was baptised at Easter, as was customary in those days, in the year 387. But he tells us almost nothing about it. It was the moment he felt his whole life had been leading up to, the moment when he felt compelled to stand up and be counted as a believer. But he doesn't describe what took place – not the words spoken, the preparations beforehand or the sharing in the Lord's supper afterwards. Nor does he explain what he thinks it all meant. All he gives us is a single sentence in which we learn that his life was changed forever: 'So we were baptised and our anxiety about our past life fled from us.'

To understand fully what that moment of baptism meant, we have to wait for the unfolding of his life as a baptised Christian. The explanations we want, the details we think we need, are not given. This means that we can't tell the story our way, we have to wait for it to emerge, as and when Augustine is ready. Until then, we can get some insights by learning to read the life he lived. His actions, choices, behaviour: these are the truest witnesses to what it meant to him, his new life 'in Christ'. In the same way, if we value our membership of the body of Christ (1 Corinthians 12:27), we should let our way of life, our actions and choices, show what our faith means to us. Because that is certainly how others will judge us, and how they will judge the faith that we profess and the Lord we serve.

Worship was a part of his life in childhood, when his mother took him (protesting, reluctant and delighted to give it up) with her to church. It became the heart of his life after his conversion and baptism. But he tells us relatively little about it, and when he does say something it is usually in passing as part of some other point he wants to make. Occasionally the joy it brings him simply bursts out of him. This is partly because his feelings about worship are that it is too precious, too important, to be shared with all and sundry. It is also true that he is talking to those who are already Christian believers and already know about it, so don't need telling. But when he comes across some difficult point, where he needs to pause and work out what he thinks, Augustine does let us have glimpses of worship and what it meant to him.

One good example of this is the case of music used in worship. We are used to thinking of singing as an essential part of how we Christians worship together. It is hard to imagine church without any singing. Some churches reduce the amount of music used in worship during Lent as a way of reminding worshippers to take it seriously as a time of self-denial, like a fast for the ears. In Augustine's time, singing in churches was just taking off as a fresh expression of worship. In addition to using the book of Psalms, people were beginning to write hymns in their own languages, expressions of what they believed, and how they felt about God.

Hymns are powerful in the way they affect us, and Augustine gave a lot of thought to the risks as well as the benefits of singing in worship. It is often said that Augustine came up with the truism, 'Anyone who sings prays twice.' He didn't ever say this, but he came pretty close when he tried to express how singing made him feel and why it was such an effective part of worship:

> The pleasures of sound captivate and enthral me more powerfully, Lord. Nowadays, I admit, I find calm contentment in the sounds which your words [of scripture] bring to life when they are sung in a pleasing and skilful voice. When words and music come together in a hymn, I feel that I ought to give it a place of honour in my heart – but I find it difficult to decide on one that is suitable. Sometimes I worry that I have a higher regard for hymns than I really should. But certainly our minds are moved in a more spiritual and passionate way by holy words when they are sung, than when they are not sung.

Augustine is not alone in being concerned about this. Christians often worry that they are confusing the medium with the message and (as it were) enjoying the attractive packaging rather than the real gift within – like children playing with a box and ignoring the present it contained. I think the best way to reassure people about this is to ask them how they would feel if they stood up to sing a favourite hymn, one which really speaks to them, and were told to sing it to the words of some other song – a nursery rhyme, perhaps, or just to sing 'la la la' instead of using words at all. Put like that, it's clear at once that the words really do matter. When we sing, the act of singing is a pleasure in its own right (even when we aren't very good singers).

But singing God's praise is a pleasure of a different kind, a far greater pleasure. Perhaps this is because, in the best hymns (like the best poetry), the words express how we feel better than we can ourselves. We have the feelings, the emotions, the belief in God, but not the skill with words to express that feeling, emotion and belief to others. When someone gives us those words, set to powerful and inspiring music, the effect can bring us to tears or bring us to our knees in thankfulness, repentance or pure, sheer joy.

Deep down, Augustine knows this, just like we do. So although he is often worried that he is allowing non-Christian elements to attract him, in the end he accepts that singing is a good thing, one of the ways by which we learn about God and draw close to God:

> At times I make the mistake of being over-anxious about this. I even wish for every tune of those soothing songs of the book of Psalms to be obliterated from my hearing and from the church. But back when I first rediscovered my faith, I remember how my tears flowed so freely when I heard your church singing. I waver between the dangers of inappropriate enjoyment and my own experience of the wholesome nature of hymn-singing. I am inclined to approve of singing in church, so that the delight it brings will inspire wavering minds to faith.

This is still important for us today, perhaps especially for Christians who find it difficult to 'let go' in worship and allow the Holy Spirit to work freely in them. Perhaps this is because they think of worship mainly as a learning and teaching opportunity, focused on the word of God being heard and explained. The way Augustine describes singing in worship soon after his baptism shows that it totally overwhelms his rational, thinking self, by filling him with joyful inspiration:

> How I wept during hymns and songs to you! How acutely was I moved by the voices of your sweet-singing church! Those voices flowed into my ears, and truth was distilled into my heart. From that, the tenderness of devotion bubbled over, and my tears flowed freely, and shedding them did me good.

Here is a man whose intellectual training pushes him towards a rational, academic approach to God. But his heart and feelings pull him another way, towards emotion, feelings and wordless ecstasy. There is room for both kinds of response in a Christian life. All of us will be drawn more strongly to one type of response rather than the other, but it is important to give due weight to the response that doesn't come so naturally to us. Sometimes we learn most when we let ourselves be taken out of that nice, safe comfort zone.

One of the reasons Christians come together to worship, and always have, right from the beginning of Christianity, is that we yearn not only to *learn* about God, but also to *experience* him. There's a funny, old-fashioned view of heaven in which people sit about on clouds with harps and halos, singing. To the outsider that sounds desperately dull. But for anyone who has experienced real worship, that funny stereotype contains a grain of true perception. For true worship is beyond description – quite literally *ecstatic* because it lifts us out of ourselves and on to another plane entirely.

So one important reason to value singing is because it is a foretaste of heaven. Another is much more practical. Singing is important and powerful, quite simply because it helps us to remember Bible teachings and Bible truths. I knew that God was 'immortal', 'invisible' and 'wise' long before I ever opened a Bible, because I sang it in a hymn at junior school. In the same way, I learned that 'God is love' and that we ought to 'praise him', and that 'Jesus loves me', because 'the Bible tells me so'.

I learned many psalms by heart through singing them week by week as part of a choir. And as I learned the words – without effort, without even trying – I gained something else as well: I took the message of the words to heart, a message rooted in the Bible, and learned to pray the words for myself. I think this kind of experience is common to most, if not all, Christians, and it is why we love hymns so much in our worship. I am sure that is why Augustine thought that singing was vitally important and ought to remain a necessary part of Christian worship.

So far I have been talking about worship as a wonderful experience, a glimpse of God, a foretaste of heaven. But, of course, it isn't always like that. Probably most of the time the reality is a long way from that kind of joy Augustine experienced at the time of his conversion.

Sometimes worship feels dull, repetitive and dry. Sometimes that is down to the place, the people and the worship leader, but sometimes the problem lies within us. Of course, worship has other jobs to do in us as well as making us joyful, uplifting us and teaching us truths about God. Worship is also there to help us put our whole life into a divine perspective – in other words to stop behaving as though we are the centre of the universe and to learn to live our lives like people for whom God is as real, and as necessary, as the air we breathe.

To understand these different ways in which worship affects us, there is one episode in Augustine's life that, for me, stands out above all the rest. That is when he tells the story of how his mother died, and how he came to terms with her death.

Augustine had a very close relationship with his mother, Monnica. They had tussles and tiffs when he was growing up, and sometimes he didn't tell her the truth, or at least not the whole truth. Sometimes (although he never explicitly says so) you get the impression that her hopes for him, her ambitions and expectations, were a suffocating burden he wanted to be rid of. It is important to say this frankly, because if this book encourages you to go and read *Confessions*, you can hardly fail to notice this.

All too often, people who write about Augustine idealise him, especially his relationship with Monnica. In reality, it was a thing of deep, abiding love, but laced with manipulation, self-interest, pressure and expectation, like most parent-child relationships. Even the effort of trying to be an ideal parent can turn into a negative. Monnica wanted her son to be a Christian. She prayed about it. She asked others to help her achieve her objective, by adding their prayers to hers. But she didn't keep this to herself. She ladled on the pressure by weeping and wailing over him, lamenting his decision to be a Manichaean instead of a proper Christian and badgering him to send his concubine away so he could marry a good Christian girl of his own class. One bishop got so fed up with her that he told her to go away and stop fussing about it. But even his dismissive words to

Monnica, 'It is impossible that the son of your tears should perish!', became, to her hopeful mind, a prophecy that in the end Augustine would become a Christian. And of course, he did.

The story of Monnica's death is interesting and moving in its own right. But one reason it's important here, as we look at what Christians today can learn from a Christian of long ago, is this: it shows us a model for how worship works, and helps, in the pressure points and crises of our everyday lives. Augustine tells the story in incredible detail, compared with other writings of that time, which weren't much interested in so-called 'ordinary' women. In *Confessions*, every detail he tells us is there for a purpose. It is not like clickbait, modern celebrity trivia to provoke our interest and manipulate us into buying something. It is meant to help us in our own faith journeys, a fact that he states openly at the end of Monnica's story. In particular, we need to be on the lookout for the way he shows how worship (public) and prayer (private) get him through the trauma and distress and help him to go on and to find comfort and peace.

We shall find out in a later chapter how, just before she died, they shared their faith, not only by talking about it but also through prayer and revelation. For now, we must imagine the scene unfolding not long after Augustine's conversion to faith. He introduces it quite simply:

> On the ninth day of her illness, when she was 56 and I was 33, that devout and faithful soul of hers was set free from the body.

Augustine's reaction to this is complicated, not least because of Monnica's own attitude to death and dying. He felt these held him to a standard that was almost impossible to endure – she didn't care about any of the things people usually worry about: where she would be buried, whether people would be able to visit the grave and tend it. She had her eyes fixed on eternal life, not on what happened to her earthly remains:

> She did not think of her corpse being elaborately laid out or embalmed; she did not crave a fine memorial or burial in her native land. Her only desire was to be remembered at your altar, where she had been devoted to you, never missing a single day.

Perhaps this should have given him comfort, given that she died in Italy, far from North Africa where he had lived most of her life. But it didn't. It was almost as if her faith was a burden to him – as sometimes happens when children feel they cannot live up to the standards set by their parents and are dogged by a sense of guilt and failure. Certainly Augustine was not up to the heroism of being glad that she was with the Lord:

> I closed her eyes. A measureless grief welled up in my heart and was on the point of overflowing into tears. At the same time, by a tremendous effort of mind my eyes suppressed their flow at its source and remained dry. The struggle to do this was so great that its effect on me was dreadful. The part of me that was still a child kept slipping into sobs, but the mature voice of my heart checked and silenced it. We were convinced that it was not right to mark the death with tearful lament and cries of sorrow, because these are the customary way to grieve at the wretchedness of the dying, or at their complete obliteration.

What we see here is a terrible conflict between the person Augustine really is and the person he thinks he ought to be. In reality, the death of his mother is crushing him with pain and grief. But he believes that this is wrong, because she is not gone forever, but 'gathered to glory'. So he feels he ought to be *glad*, because she is receiving the reward for her faith. Theory is one thing; practice is something quite different. Christians, he feels, have nothing to fear from death. So why is he utterly bereft?

One small clue is there in the words he uses. He speaks of '*my* eyes' holding back tears and the 'voice of *my* heart' trying to argue him out of weeping. Then comes a switch to the plural – '*we*' thought it was wrong to be unhappy at her death. That change from 'I' to 'we' points us to one of the great pressures to which all Christians are prone: the judgement of other people. Specifically, their negative judgement of us, their disapproval and criticism.

It is hard enough living the Christian life as it is, without adding an extra layer of pressure by trying to live up to other people's expectations, especially if those expectations have very little to do with what God himself wants from us. It is normal and natural to care what other people think of us, but not when it makes us force ourselves into unnatural ways of thinking and behaving. This is even more so when what makes us do what we believe to be right is a fear of being judged rather than a genuine personal commitment to a belief.

This problem about death was something Augustine shared with other Christians of his time. They lived in an era when there was no concept of, not even a word for, what we call psychology. The idea that human beings might be subject to feelings and emotions without needing to categorise them as 'good' or 'bad' was unfamiliar. They were also likely to think that emotions were dangerous and needed to be regulated and controlled.

Saying that emotion was natural was not the same thing, back then, as saying it was 'good' or even 'inevitable'. For them grief wasn't a state of mind, it was a *choice*. Augustine's Christian beliefs taught him that death was not an evil, so this is how he forces himself to understand Monnica's death:

> Her dying did not happen in a pitiable way, and she was not utterly annihilated. We believed this on the evidence of her manner of life, her unfeigned faith and our firm convictions.

Not all his cleverness, though, was enough to reason himself out of his grief. I remember back in the days when I was still a smoker,

I tried both reason and prayer as a way to rid me of my craving for nicotine. Neither worked. Reason didn't work, because I didn't smoke because of reasons; I smoked because I was addicted. Prayer didn't work because – I now understand – in reality I was trying to offload the responsibility. I had a choice, but I wanted to be set free from the responsibility of deciding to smoke. Thankfully nicotine patches saw me through in the end.

There is no shortcut to getting over grief, because grief is as natural to us as hunger and tiredness. When we are grieved, we have to accept it and deal with it. We cannot reason it away. It can be a hard lesson for Christians who think that with prayer and right thinking they can be whatever they want to be, instead of the imperfect, weak person they really are. Pride is a big obstacle here. It made Augustine's dilemma worse because he was afraid of being found out, of being too weak a Christian to be glad at his mother's death instead of sorrowful. With typical honesty, he asks himself, and God, why the pain of his bereavement is so terrible:

> What was it, then, which caused such great pain within me? Was it perhaps the fresh wound inflicted by our habitual way of life together – so dear and precious as it was – being suddenly ripped apart?

There is another clue here to help us understand his difficulty. He is doing what we all do when we are afraid that we are not on the right track, or when we are overcome by doubts: in order to reassure ourselves that we are thinking right, we try to persuade others to follow our point of view, because if we can succeed we will have proof that we were right all along. Augustine does just that – he tries to impose the principles about which he has inward doubts and qualms on to others, as a way of bolstering his own belief. Desperate to give way to grief himself, he and his friends stop his son from expressing his sorrow through crying:

> After we had checked Adeodatus' sobs, Evodius took up a psalter and began to sing a psalm. The whole household responded as one: 'I shall sing of your mercy and justice, O Lord' [Psalm 101:1].

In effect, they are teaching Adeodatus to adopt a standard of behaviour, even though inside themselves they know they are failing to live up to that standard. Teaching others becomes a way of running away from the truth. Being the exceptionally self-aware person he was, Augustine can't help noticing this flaw, and he admits to God, in his *Confessions*, that he is showing one face to the world and quite another in his grief-filled isolation:

> Those who were listening carefully to me, and thought I had no sense of grief, were quite unaware of the torment I was enduring. In your hearing, Lord, I reproached myself for the weakness of my feelings, and I restrained the flow of lamentation, and it receded a little. Then once more it attacked me with full force, not to the point of breaking into sobs, nor to a change in my outward expression – but I was aware of what feeling I was crushing in my heart… and I was torn apart by this twofold distress.

When he describes Monnica's funeral – her body being carried from the house and then the cremation – he draws attention to his lack of any outward signs of distress. This would have been unusual among non-Christians at a funeral, where weeping and wailing was the norm, an expected part of the process of death and funerals. We can sense the guilt and shame he felt that he was failing by both standards – the Christian refusal to grieve and the public and visible non-Christian laments:

> When her body was carried out, we left the house and returned afterwards without any tears. Nor did we weep during the prayers… beside the tomb, where the body was laid prior to burial. Not even during those prayers did I shed a tear. Yet all

that day I was secretly crushed with grief, and in a turmoil of mind I asked you continually, as best I could, to heal my pain. You did not do so.

Anyone reading this who has ever tried to use prayer to overcome their own deep-seated habits or feelings (as I did with smoking), and to make themselves into someone they are not, will sympathise with Augustine's suffering here. That suffering did come to an end, but not through passage of time or persuasive argument, not even through prayer. In an extraordinary turnaround, his grief was transformed and set free through the memory of worship. When he tells us how this came about, it becomes easy to see why he decided not to oppose hymn-singing in church. Because it was the experience of such singing, called to mind in a moment of personal crisis, that allowed him to find peace and solace, without disguise and without pretence:

I slept, and awoke, and discovered that my pain was markedly lessened. As I lay in bed alone I called to mind that hymn written by your servant Ambrose, which spoke truly:

O God, the maker of all things,
You rule the heavens, and you clothe
The day with light magnificent,
The night with drowsy-making grace:
So that a time of ease restores
Our rested limbs to do their work,
Lightens the cares of wearied minds,
And frees our anxious hearts from grief.

Waking to fresh hope; trusting in God's creative power and goodness; remembering God's promise to liberate human beings from grief – all this comes to him as he lies in bed at the dawn of a new day. This is not the moment when he somehow talked himself into being happy. He had tried that already, and it had failed. This is the moment when he felt God had given him permission to be honest, to speak his mind and to express his heart:

From then on, Lord, it was a comfort to weep about my mother, and for her, about myself and for myself, in your presence. I let flow my tears, which I had until that moment restrained, and let them fall as freely as they would. I made them a bed to rest my heart upon; and it did find rest on them, since my sobs were for your ears only, not for any harsh interpreter to hear. Now, Lord, I make my confession to you in writing. Let anyone read it who will, let them interpret as they will.

He hasn't entirely lost his fear of other people's bad opinions. He is still thinking of how people will judge him for this change of heart. But he has realised that he cannot let such judgements dictate his own reaction to Monnica's death. God is okay with him grieving and weeping for her – and to Augustine, given permission through his memories of worship, nothing else matters:

If readers do find fault, they shouldn't be scornful because I wept so briefly for my mother who was, at least for the present, dead to my sight – and who had wept over me for so many years, Lord, in the hope that I would come to live in your sight.

As he looks back on that time of bereavement when writing his *Confessions*, Augustine speaks across the centuries to everyone who reads them, and he asks them to join him in praying for his mother, and his father, so that her last request to him (to remember her at Holy Communion) may be fulfilled through all his readers, not by himself alone:

O my Lord, my God, inspire your servants, whenever they read my Confessions, to remember at your altar your servant Monnica and her sometime husband Patricius. Let her last request to me be fulfilled for her more abundantly through many people's prayers – prompted by my Confessions – than by my prayers alone.

So Augustine learns to worship, and discovers the power of praying together with other Christians. He brings the distant past right into our present, by asking us, when we hear his story, to pray with him.

Bible passage for reflection

When the Lord restored the fortunes of Zion,
    we were like those who dream.
Then our mouth was filled with laughter,
    and our tongue with shouts of joy;
then it was said among the nations,
    'The Lord has done great things for them.'
The Lord has done great things for us,
    and we rejoiced.

Restore our fortunes, O Lord,
    like the watercourses in the Negeb.
May those who sow in tears
    reap with shouts of joy.
Those who go out weeping,
    bearing the seed for sowing,
shall come home with shouts of joy,
    carrying their sheaves.

PSALM 126

Like many of the psalms in the Bible, this one has a title. That title tells us that it was a song for people to sing on their way to Jerusalem, as they were climbing up to the temple. It is a short song and full of joy. The people have been through a time of suffering, but the Lord has brought them through it, and their present state is like a beautiful dream. This change of fortunes is like water coming to a dry land; the crops are sown in doubt and despair, but the harvest is abundant. The message is manifold, but the point I draw from it now is an obvious one (though not too obvious to need stating) – life and worship go together. God is woven into the fabric of our lives, whether or not we are aware of it. But if and when we do become aware of his presence, our life becomes infinitely better and more blessed once we respond to him, through worship with fellow Christians, those who share in our pilgrimage. Life and worship are not about everything being easy. But they are about trust that in the end all shall be well.

Questions

1 What is our worship meant to do for us?
2 Why does God want our worship?
3 Can you think of a time when worship has given you answers or comfort that you could not find anywhere else?
4 Does it matter what other people think of us when we are worshipping together?
5 Why does singing matter so much to Christians?
6 Are our fellow Christians ever more of a hindrance than a help when we are worshipping together?

Prayer

Lord God, let my whole life be a sacrifice of praise;
a sacrifice made willingly,
and even joyfully;
because when I am with my fellow Christians,
and my heart is ready for praise,
there is nowhere I would rather be,
and nothing I would rather be doing,
because you are my Alpha and my Omega,
my Beginning and my End. Amen

7

Augustine learns to pray alone

By now, we have learned quite a lot about Augustine and his faith. But we are about to go even deeper, into his actual encounters with God. In the Bible, we are used to people having such encounters with God; for example, Isaiah (6:1–5), Daniel (7:9–11) and Ezekiel (1:25–28). Moses talks with God face to face, as one talks with a friend (cf. Deuteronomy 34:10). Jesus speaks directly to God as a way of showing his disciples how they can talk to God too. Peter, James and John get a glimpse of Jesus' true divine nature at the transfiguration (Matthew 17:2; Mark 9:3; Luke 9:29; 2 Peter 1:16). Stephen sees the heavens opened at the very moment when he is being martyred (Acts 7:55). The Bible ends with a long description of the vision of John of Patmos.

If you work your way through all these visions, and weigh them up and compare them, one thing that immediately strikes you is that none of them describes what God looks like. His surroundings are described, as is the effect of his presence (such as light and glory), but God himself is not. As the Bible is the only firm guide to what real vision is, I think we have to take it from this that true visions do not show us what God looks like.

My own experience, limited as it is, bears this out. I have used meditation on the life of Jesus as a way to pray for many years, and I have taught it to individuals and occasionally to groups of Christians. But in every gospel scene I take as the basis for my meditation, I have never seen the face of Christ. I can imagine the scenery in detail, the people, the noises, the scent of the air, the movement. But not the face of Jesus, not ever. Sometimes his back, but never his face.

Not all Bible visions are described in the same way. Sometimes they are said to be 'like a dream'. This is not because they are imaginary or unreal; it is because the person describing them is aware that their encounter with God stands outside the realm of normal human experience. Another word often used is 'revelation', which comes from a Latin word meaning 'unveiling' – in other words, showing clearly something that once had been hidden. The Greek word for this 'unveiling', also well-known, is 'apocalypse'.

Visions, dreams, revelations: all of these belong to the world of the individual human being and the God who reaches out to them. They are not part of church worship, when Christians come together. They are a different, individual, personal encounter with the living God. And that makes some Christians, especially church leaders, uneasy about them. There is always the possibility that someone is making a power play, claiming vision as a way of attracting followers not for God but for themselves. Visions are not subject to authority; there is no quality control. This means we have to be careful, and apply the gospel test Jesus recommends: 'you will know them by their fruits' (Matthew 7:20).

We have seen the effect that Christian worship had on Augustine as a new Christian. It is now time to discover what happened to him when he finally let go of his doubts, and let God in, from the angle of his personal prayer life. I've just said that we need to be cautious about people who claim to have had visions. One of the tests we can apply is how easily they talk about their vision. Sometimes it can take years before they feel comfortable sharing anything of their experience. Probably a great many visions go unrecorded because the people who have them never share them with another living soul. Talking about our lives of personal prayer isn't easy.

We are going to discover how Augustine came to experience vision, or revelation, in his prayers. But we need to understand first that not all experiences of God in private prayer come in the shape of something we can see or hear. Often, they come in the shape of what I can best describe as a 'moment of clarity' – an insight into God's nature or our situation. Sometimes when I am talking to students about difficult choices and decisions, I suggest that they go and sit in chapel (as a way of consciously putting themselves in God's path) and tell him what's on their mind, and then wait. No words may be heard. No vision may be seen. But still they often leave the chapel at peace and with a fresh clear sense of direction, a vision if you like, of what to do next or how to handle the difficulty that has been weighing them down.

Augustine's life is full of such moments. But the older he became, and the more bogged down with running the church and battling for true Christian belief, the less he tells us about visions and glimpses of glory. So we can't tell if he still had them in his later years. This too is true to how vision seems to work in people's lives. They get the vision *when they need it*, and then it is gone. And they, as it were, feed off it to sustain them in the task God has called them to do. We see this with Peter's vision of the clean and unclean food or Paul's mysterious vision (actually an 'audition', as it was heard, not seen) on the road to Damascus – both apostles come back to their visions again and again, as they try to make sense of them and use them for the good of other people (Peter: Acts 10:9–16, 28; 11:5–10; Paul: Acts 9:3–19; 22:6–21; 26:12–18). The vision of Jesus transfigured is like that – Peter, James and John get just a momentary glimpse, and then it is gone. Visions are not to be chased. We are not supposed to try to recreate the experience. We are supposed to put it to work.

So what we learn of the private prayer life Augustine enjoyed mostly comes from what he wrote early in his life as a Christian. He tells us a lot in *Confessions* about his insights on God's nature and his own human condition. And then we have to guess that he put those insights to work in the considerably less glamorous world of ordinary human living and daily decision-making. We can learn a lot from his glimpses of truth, his 'mini-visions', for want of a better way of describing them. They come thick and fast in the early books of *Confessions*. Remember that he is always talking directly to God – which makes *Confessions* a special kind of extended vision or revelation in its own right. Here he is telling God about how he feels he is being pulled in two directions, towards God and towards his ordinary human existence (a feeling that many Christians will share):

> Sometimes you draw me deep within, into an experience like no other, to an inexplicable pleasure. If that pleasure were perfected in me, I do not know what could possibly be lacking from such a life. But I am weighed down and encumbered, and fall back into this existence, and I am sucked back into accustomed ways, and stuck fast. However much I weep, I am still held back. So much for the value of the burden of habit! I have strength enough to exist here on earth, but wish I did not. I want to be in that other place, but have not the strength for it. In both respects I am pitiable.

He feels torn apart by the competing voices of God, on the one hand, and human existence, on the other. His Christian principles clash with his human instincts, and he does not know how to handle that clash. And yet he remains convinced that God is reachable somehow and that God has made it possible for human beings to know something of who he is. In one famous passage, he expresses his feelings about God at some length and manages to tie together all the things that God is *not* with everything that he *is*:

> Highest, best, most powerful, most omnipotent, most merciful and most just, most hidden and most evident, most beautiful and most sovereign; steadfast and inconceivable; unchanging yet changing all things; never new, never old; renewing all things… Always active, always at rest; uniting and needing nothing; bringing and filling and protecting; creating and nurturing and bringing to perfection; seeking even though you

lack nothing. You love, yet do not burn with passion; you are zealous in your love and yet peaceable; you repent without regretting; you are angry yet serene; you change your works yet do not change your purpose; you accept what you find and have never lost… Who owns anything that is not, in reality, yours? After all this, what have we said, my God, my life, my holy sweetness?

The words and images come thick and fast. But at the end of them he has to admit that he has still failed to encapsulate God, for the simple reason that it is impossible to do so. This is a good example of why trying to express visions in words is so difficult, even though what Augustine writes here makes me glad that he did his best! God is beyond it all – 'above all and through all and in all' (Ephesians 4:6).

Augustine has a long way to go, and a lot of growing up to do, before he reaches this kind of prayer. It is quite reassuring to read what he says about how his prayer life began, because it will sound familiar to most of us:

I was still a boy when I began to pray to you, Lord. When I was a small child, I begged you with all my heart not to let me be beaten at school. Then, when (to prevent my foolishness) you did not grant my request, my elders and even my parents (who had no desire to see any harm befall me) laughed at the marks of my beatings. But to me they were a grim and weighty evil.

It is hard for me, as a parent, to imagine ever laughing at the marks of a child's beating at school. It makes clear how different Augustine's world was from ours. But that first effort at prayer is typical of where people's prayer life begins: 'Lord, give me something I want; save me from something I fear!' This is where prayer begins, but it cannot stay there if the Christian's life is to flourish and develop.

Note the maturity with which Augustine deals with the problem of God not giving him what he asks for. It is not that God hasn't heard or hasn't answered, but that he has answered 'no' to stop Augustine's foolishness. Perhaps it was foolish of him to pray not to be beaten at school, but it was entirely natural and not wrong. We are not to sit around debating what to put in front of God so that he can select out whatever he decides to say 'yes' to. Instead, we are to take our needs to him even though they may be trivial and insignificant, because at that moment, trivial or not, that is where we are, and they are what is on our mind. And that is all that matters.

Augustine's life of prayer ranges from what is day-to-day and trivial to some of the most intense, extraordinary experiences he has ever had. He is comfortable speaking to God in a straightforward conversational way; *Confessions* is, from start to finish, just such a conversation. But he also uses repeated prayers, which he has learned by heart during worship and knows from the gospels.

Not surprisingly, the most important of these are the psalms and the Lord's Prayer. When giving advice on the basics of Christian living, Augustine says that daily praying of the Lord's Prayer is all we need to deal with the inevitable trivial sins of daily life. He thinks of this prayer as blotting out small everyday sins altogether. I think this is because taking Jesus' words in that prayer and making them our words too is a way of 'being on the Lord's side', of trying to be Christlike. By saying this prayer every day, we are seeking to comfort and strengthen ourselves, not to inform God, as Augustine says in another passage. God knows everything already, but we still need to put our needs into words for him. Sometimes Augustine explains the Lord's Prayer in a more detailed way:

> The Lord's Prayer in Matthew's gospel contains seven requests. Three ask for eternal things, the other four for earthly things. So when we say, 'Hallowed be thy name. Thy Kingdom come. Thy will be done on earth, as it is in heaven,' these are blessings we will keep forever – they begin here, then they progress in us and grow, and once perfected in the life to come they are ours forever. But when we say, 'Give us this day our daily bread.

And forgive us our debts, as we forgive our debtors. And lead us
not into temptation, but deliver us from evil,' it is obvious that
these requests relate to our needs in this life.

So for Augustine this prayer is a perfect balance between our
spiritual needs and our physical needs, and as such it ought to have
a unique value to all Christians. Praying it should never descend into
the kind of 'vain repetitions' Jesus is so critical of in the sermon on
the mount (Matthew 6:7, KJV).

All Christians learn from their fellow Christians how to live and
behave as Christians and what being a Christian really means.
This was also true for Augustine. Throughout his childhood and
adolescence and into early adulthood, he had the example of his
mother's faith, which clearly made a big impact on him even though
he couldn't accept it intellectually. At one point, while Augustine was
a Manichaean, his mother seriously considered throwing him out of
home because of his way of life. But she had a vision, and as a result
decided not to:

Where did that dream come from, after all, by which you
consoled her, Lord, so that she let me live with her and have my
meals with her at home? She had become reluctant to allow this
because she loathed and detested my blasphemy and heresy.
She saw herself standing upon a kind of wooden ruler and a
glorious young man coming towards her smiling cheerfully
at her, though she herself was sorrowful and overcome with
grief. When the youth asked her the reasons for her sorrow and
her daily weeping, she replied that she was lamenting the fact
that I was damned. At this, to reassure her, he told her most
solemnly to observe that where she was, there I was also. As
soon as she heard this, she saw me standing beside her on the
same ruler.

Monnica shared this vision with her son, presumably while explaining
why she wasn't kicking him out after all. It wasn't the only time she

had a vision, either. Augustine mentions other occasions when she felt that she was being taken into a different realm of being. And uniquely (at least I have never come across anything like it in my experience or in my reading), they shared a vision together. I will turn to that vision in a moment. Before that, I want to look at the first time Augustine had a vision of his own – how it happened and why.

We have seen already how Augustine gradually overcame his doubts about the Bible as a source of truth. It took time. He needed to read, and he had to think through a lot of issues. At one point, he compared the Bible message with what he had read in philosophy books. Both spoke of God as creator and of a divine Word, but only the Bible spoke of God's Word becoming a human being and living among us. Only the Bible spoke of Christ Jesus voluntarily giving up his equality with God to take on human likeness. And only the Bible said that he died on the cross, not just for the righteous but for the unrighteous too.

While he compares the two sources of wisdom, weighing up these two ways of understanding God, he is taking the Bible 100% seriously for the first time. He is approaching it with the right kind of attitude: not snobbery or scepticism, but honest inquiry and hunger for truth. And at that point, that very moment, he experiences a vision of the Truth (John 14:6):

> I entered deep within myself under your guidance, Lord, for you became my helper. I entered and saw, as it were with the eye of my soul, above that same eye of my soul, and above my mind, the unchangeable Light. It was not this ordinary light which all human beings can behold. Nor was it a grander version of the same kind of thing. That light was something else, something utterly different. It was not above my mind in the way that oil floats above water, or sky above land. It was greater than that, because it made me, and I was lesser because I was its creation. Anyone who knows the Truth knows this light; and anyone who knows it knows eternity too. Love knows it.

Reading his words so many centuries afterwards, there is a real sense of excitement and immediacy. There is a simplicity, a certainty, that what he is experiencing is real. It is so powerful that, even though time has passed and he was writing from an alien culture and in a foreign language, we feel close to him, privileged to have an insight into his deepest spiritual experience. Even so, it is hard for us to imagine what that must have been like. We would like to know a lot more about the circumstances. Where was he at the time? What time of day did it take place? How did the Lord give him the guidance he refers to? How on earth are we supposed to imagine a light utterly unlike ordinary light? And what happened afterwards – how did he come back down to earth?

Perhaps that is beyond most of us. But the fact that we can't grasp all the details doesn't mean we can't believe what we are being told. And the way Augustine talks about it is, for me, utterly compelling. Truth. Light. Eternity. Love. The words for expressing God come thick and fast; all are biblical and totally convincing. But unless we ourselves have experienced something like this, entering into the reality of Augustine's vision is surely beyond us. We have to make do with his description of it. And that's okay. Arguably, God gives visions only to those who need them. If we have not had that experience, it could be because God judges us not to need it. Certainly, those moments of vision made a huge difference to how God overcame Augustine's stubborn resistance to the gospel. The love and relief spill out of him in words of such joy that they still take my breath away, even though I have read them and thought about them many times:

> O eternal Truth, and true Love, and beloved Eternity, you are my God – day and night I sigh for you! When I first recognised you, you lifted me up to show me that there was something I must see, but I was not yet capable of seeing it. Your beams of light reflected back the weakness of my sight, so brightly did they shine upon me, and I trembled with love and awe. You called from far off, 'Truly I am who I am.' And I heard you, as one

hears in one's heart, and from that moment there was no room for doubt, and I would sooner doubt that I was alive than that Truth was non-existent, for it is visible and understood through the things that have been made.

These are words of love, spoken at that time of first rapture, in all the delight of passion and commitment. It was the start of a lifelong love affair with God. Now we can begin to see how it came about that he was finally able to let go of his old life, which he had thought himself incapable of turning his back on. No human relationship could compare with this love – not his love for his mother or his partner or even his son. It is wonderful to read of such pure joy in someone's relationship with God. Perhaps we may feel a twinge of regret that our own relationship with him is not so passionate, not so rewarding. If that is the case, well, the solution is in our own hands. Augustine was never a man for half measures. If he was going to become a Christian, he was going to commit himself to it body and soul. It is as true of our relationship with God as of everything else in life, that what we get out depends on what we are prepared to put in.

That was Augustine's first vision. There may have been many others, perhaps even throughout his long life. I get the feeling that he only tells us about the ones he thinks we *need* to know about. I am glad that he decided we needed to know about another vision he had – because there is nothing else quite like it in the whole of Christian history. I think it helps to give us the measure of the man and a real sense of the incredible power of his faith and his insight into God.

Not long before his mother Monnica died, the two of them were standing at a window looking out into a garden, resting after a time of travel. They were talking together normally, when suddenly everyday reality gave way to a moment of revelation, as the veil between this earthly realm and God's eternity was drawn back – and drawn back not just for Augustine, but for both of them, as they experienced a vision together.

When we look at what he tells us about it, we shall find that it has the same markers of truth about it as his other visions. But there is an additional aspect of wonder about it, created by its being shared between them. As stated earlier, when God grants people a moment of vision, it is not as a reward for good behaviour or loyal service. It is because they need the strength it gives them for a job they have to do. That is certainly true of the visions in the Bible we glanced at earlier; it is also true, I think, of this one. Though neither Augustine nor Monnica realised it at the time, the vision was preparing them both for the moment when they must be parted. And by sharing it with us, through writing it down for future generations of Christians, Augustine is encouraging us to use it to strengthen ourselves, so that we can live as people who truly believe in the reality of God in this life and in the life of the world to come.

As he leads up to the vision itself, he tells us that God has brought about the moment, the time and the place, making it clear that everything is in his hands:

> The day was now at hand, Lord, when she was to depart this life – a day which you already knew, though the two of us did not. By your own mysterious ways you brought it about that she and I were standing alone, leaning at a particular window where there was a prospect over the garden within the house where we were staying. We were far away from the crowds, recovering from the stress of a long journey and making ready for the onward voyage. So we were conversing with pleasure, just the two of us, 'forgetting the past but rather reaching out to what is to come' [Philippians 3:13].

They are discussing together how to make sense of eternal life. It's the sort of discussion two Christian people might have at any time, but the fact that Monnica died so soon afterwards adds a poignancy for Augustine as he looks back on that moment years later. Sometimes the pattern and direction in our lives and the meaning behind events, takes years, even decades, to emerge. Mother and son are not trying to impress one another with their faith; it is not a contest of competitive piety. Neither are they trying to reassure themselves, by professing outward beliefs about which they have inward doubts. As Augustine describes it, one moment they are having a normal, if intense, conversation, and the next moment they are lifted out of themselves (the true meaning of the word 'ecstasy') and are being carried into another realm, another way of being (perhaps in the way that Paul writes about in 2 Corinthians 12:2), to behold truths that are beyond description, never mind understanding:

> In the presence of the Truth (which is who you really are, Lord) we were exploring the question of what the eternal life of the saints would be like, which 'eye has not seen nor ear heard nor has it entered into the human heart'. We opened wide the mouth of our heart to drink deeply of the heavenly waters of your pure spring, the 'well of life' that abides with you. Then we were sprinkled to the limit of our poor ability and thus began to reflect widely on this great matter.

The water he refers to is partly the water of life referred to in the Bible (Revelation 22:1, 17) and partly water used as a sign of purification. They are being prepared for an encounter for which they cannot possibly be worthy or, as we might say, which they cannot possibly deserve. That too is a marker of a true vision – Isaiah's first reaction, when he has his vision of God, is dismay at his own unworthiness (Isaiah 6:5). Augustine and Monnica have just agreed on the main point, that physical joys and pleasures are worthless in comparison with the joys of eternal life, and at that moment they are suddenly no longer two earthly human beings standing in a garden in a town in north Italy; they are taken out of themselves and into another realm entirely:

> We raised ourselves up and, with hearts aflame for the One, we made our gradual ascent through the physical world and even heaven itself, where sun and moon and stars shine upon the earth.

'The One', of course, refers to God. Augustine sees God as a perfect unity, in contrast to humanity, which is broken and flawed. The heaven he passes through is the sky above the earth, which he thinks of as a different place from heaven as the place where the righteous abide for ever:

> Now we were climbing still further, and pondering, discussing and marvelling at your works. We entered into our own minds and transcended them, to reach that place of unfailing abundance, where you feed your people forever with the food of truth. There, life is the wisdom by which all other things come to be, both past and future – wisdom that is not created, but rather exists just as it always has been and always will be. In fact, it does not have the capacity either to *have* existed or to *come to* exist. It simply is, because it is eternal.

We notice straightaway that he describes this experience as being like climbing a mountain. That should come as no surprise – in the Bible, mountains are often places where people go to find God or sometimes where they meet God unexpectedly. Moses finds God on Horeb (Exodus 3:1). Zion is the dwelling place of God in the Old Testament. Jesus goes up a mountain when he wants to pray (Matthew 14:23), and he is on a mountain when the transfiguration happens (Matthew 17:1), and Peter, James and John get a privileged glimpse of him as he truly is, the eternal Word, the Son of God.

What Augustine means by 'entered into their own minds' is much more puzzling. I think that perhaps he was imagining them as somehow journeying into their own nature, exploring their identity as Christians and as human beings. One thing is clear, though: they leave behind that ordinary, self-centred identity and nature as they come close, so close, to God, and – for a little while – enter heaven itself.

The vision is a joy and a wonder. To read about it is striking enough. To have experienced it is extraordinary, unimaginable. But it is not a place where either of them is allowed to stay. Not yet. There can be no remaining in that state of ecstasy. The world is not to be run away from, but engaged with, and the two of them must return to ordinary life, albeit strengthened in their faith, hope and love, by what they have seen and heard:

> While we spoke, we also gazed upon wisdom with longing; we reached out and touched it as best we could, with every beat of our heart. Then we sighed and left behind us, where they belonged, those first fruits of the Spirit. We returned to the din of our ordinary speech, in which words have both beginnings and endings. Yet what can compare with your Word, our Lord, who is everlasting, never ageing, yet making all things new?

The way Augustine writes about this double vision (so to speak) shows how hard it is for him to put his experience into words. That is often the way with our experiences of God, too. We are taken out of our comfort zone, out of the life we know, and given some brief glimpse, some small experience, of a new way of being. But it is easier to live life the old familiar way – habits can be very hard to break! When he tries to explain the difference between everyday ways of talking and this vision of the Word, he finds even his brilliance as a writer falls short. No words can do justice to the Word. All he can do is describe his joy and wonder and admit that the puzzle is beyond his ability to make sense of. He admits this quite openly, when he teaches new Christians about how to pray and recommends silent prayer:

> What delights me more, and sticks with me, is what I see in silence in my mind. I am very reluctant to be dragged away from this to the inferior cacophony of words.

This reminds me of the famous saying attributed to Francis of Assisi: 'Preach Jesus. If necessary, use words.'

Bible passage for reflection

> As an apple tree among the trees of the wood,
>   so is my beloved among young men.
> With great delight I sat in his shadow,
>   and his fruit was sweet to my taste.
> He brought me to the banqueting house,
>   and his intention towards me was love.
>
> SONG OF SONGS 2:3–4

Our personal relationship with God needs as much energy, effort and commitment as all our other relationships. We cannot get the most out of it if we neglect our beloved Lord. In this passage of the Bible our relationship with God is described in terms of the love between a man and a woman. Each is totally absorbed in the other, each finds every aspect of the other entrancing, delightful. Above all, that relationship is *fulfilling*: it gives us a joy that nothing else can. As such, it is also *fruitful*: it has a positive effect not only on us, but also on all those around us. Our love for God is deeply personal. But it can never, should never, be private.

Questions

1 How did you first learn to pray?
2 Have you ever tried to teach anyone else to pray?
3 Why does God show himself to us only rarely in our personal prayers?
4 How do you prepare yourself for prayer, and what have you discovered through experience are the most helpful ways to pray alone?
5 Do you pray enough?

Prayer

Lord God, I am not as ready to pray as you are to hear me;
I am not as honest as I could be;
I often hurry through my times of prayer.
But I am your servant, just the same,
and I want to do better in the future than I have done in the past,
and learn to love you more nearly day by day.
So help me, Lord, to make my good intentions real. Amen

8

Augustine talking about God: beauty, light, truth

There is more than one way of talking about God and more than one way of talking to God. There is not one right way; everything depends on the person we are and how we feel able to connect with God. By now, we have discovered what a complicated person Augustine was. He was clever, yet sometimes extremely slow on the uptake. He was self-controlled, yet passionate; full of desires, yet uninterested in many types of temptation. He was a brilliant speaker and writer, yet disappointed with his failure to put his feelings about God, and his understanding of God, into words.

In public, Augustine was a bishop, a leader in the church and in society, an intellectual giant; in private, he was often needy of reassurance, guidance and affirmation. The public man taught what he believed God and the Bible revealed to him: a world where judgement could be passed on a whole class of people, even a whole nation, for the failings of a few; the private Christian was utterly convinced that God demands only that we do everything from the motive of Christian love and that God judges us by this standard not as a group ('Christians' or 'the church'), but as individual human beings. Our relationship with God is fundamentally personal, not impersonal or general.

If people know anything about Augustine before they read *Confessions* or start to learn about him, it is likely to be one of these key things:

1 His famous prayer, 'Make me virtuous and chaste, Lord, but not just yet!'
2 His other famous prayer, 'Lord, you have made us for yourself, and our hearts are restless until they rest in you.'
3 He taught something called 'original sin'.

Unlike various quotes falsely attributed to Augustine, both the prayers are indeed his words. Both come from *Confessions*, and both reveal a genuine person with all the complicated and contradictory instincts that we ourselves have. The background to original sin is a bit more complicated; it is linked to some of the arguments that took place between Augustine and Pelagius. Pelagius denied original or birth sin. He thought that we come into the world pure and free from sin and are gradually corrupted by our living in the world. Augustine would have agreed completely that life in this world exposes us to all sorts of sin. But he knew that the only reason sin affects us is our inborn inability to resist doing wrong. And that is not something we just pick up as life goes along; it is fundamental to who we are.

Original sin doesn't mean inventing some type of misbehaviour which no one's thought of before! Sin is by nature boring, predictable and repetitive, and it always has been, throughout human history. Rather, the concept of original sin was a way of explaining why human beings seem utterly incapable of choosing the right path, even when they know what it is – as Paul says, 'I do not do the good I want, but the evil I do not want is what I do' (Romans 7:19).

Augustine had no knowledge of modern science, biology, genetics or physics, and he believed that the story of Adam and Eve in Genesis was real history. So he made the connection between the first thing that human beings did wrong (the 'original' sin) and their ongoing sinfulness and argued that it was a flaw transmitted from one generation to the next, as each parent begets each child. Because Adam sinned, all of us are incapable of avoiding sin (Romans 5:15; see also 1 Corinthians 15:45). To strengthen his case, Augustine referred to a verse that seemed to bear out his take on the origin of sin: 'Indeed, I was born guilty, a sinner when my mother conceived me' (Psalm 51:5).

Like Paul before him, and like so many of us afterwards, Augustine was frustrated by his own inability to be what he saw God wanted him to be. As Paul wrote: 'I see in my members [or 'body'] another law at war with the law of my mind, making me captive to the law of sin that dwells in my members' (Romans 7:23).

There are two reasons why this matters here. One is that a lot of people are critical of Augustine because they have heard of his ideas on original sin, and don't like them. Of course, it is a lot easier to criticise those ideas than to come up with something equally biblical and convincing. The other reason is that it proves to us (if we needed convincing) that Augustine did not shy away from teaching a doctrine just because it was hard.

This helps us to be sure that he is never preaching down to us. Whatever he tells us about God and human beings, and about his own spiritual experience, comes from the perspective of someone who can say, hand on heart, 'Lord… I am not worthy to have you come under my roof' (Luke 7:6). For him, the life of prayer and learning is not a self-improvement course in which we gradually improve our skills and get better at being Christians. It is about a relationship rooted in messy human reality, which God enters, to transform it.

In this chapter, we meet Augustine the poet. He was not a poet in the sense of someone who writes verse and rhyme, but rather in the sense of someone who uses language to the absolute utmost of his ability (which in his case was quite something) to try to express the wonder of God. I have chosen those passages from his writings that speak to me most directly about how it feels to be in touch with God and attuned to God. There are plenty of others, and the best way to find them is to read *Confessions*. But the passages I have chosen speak to me because (I can't prove this, but I think I am right) they put into words the fruits of his visions, which we looked at in the previous chapter. Sometimes it can be difficult to see why they are so special – after all, plenty of other writers try to put their personal love for God into words! But Augustine was the pioneer: the first person outside the Bible to talk about God and to God and to share with others his journey into faith by writing it as a step-by-step account. He sets the standard, and all the rest follow in his wake.

The passages I have chosen speak of three ways of understanding God. All of them were important to Augustine. All of them can still help and guide us today.

One passage stands out above all others, even in the huge quantity of his writings we have available to us. It comes from *Confessions*, from a point where Augustine has accepted the Christian God and Christian truth, has been baptised and has begun to turn his thoughts to some of the big questions about how to live as a Christian. How should he try to turn a moment's decision and an ongoing inclination into a lifetime of true discipleship?

Just before the passage in question, Augustine has been exploring how we can learn about God from looking at the world he has made, and he shows us how God's hand is visible in all his works. Then Augustine turns to the five senses – hearing, sight, smell, taste and touch – and how we can use them and understand them as tools in our search for God. Although all of them can be misdirected to sinful ends, they are all good things in themselves, gifts from God meant to help us find our way to him. The most extraordinary thing in these wonderful words is Augustine's insight that above everything else God is *beautiful* – indeed he even calls him by that name. I will let the words speak for themselves, before saying any more:

> Late have I loved you, O Beauty so old and so new: late have I
>   loved you!
> And look! You were within me, and I was outside myself:
> and it was there that I searched for you.

In my unloveliness I plunged into the lovely things
    which you created:
you were with me, but I was not with you.
Those created things kept me far away from you:
yet if they had not been in you, they would have not been at all.
You called and shouted: and broke through my deafness.
You flamed and shone: and banished my blindness.
You breathed your fragrance on me:
and I drew in my breath and I pant for you.
I have tasted you: and now I hunger and thirst for more.
You have touched me: and I have burned for your peace.

How does it make you feel to read that? It makes me feel humble; and, if I'm honest, a bit envious. I wish my relationship with God was as deep and glorious as that! But perhaps it is those who have once fallen furthest away who have the deepest appreciation of God's beauty and love. Clothed in these wonderful words, Augustine is trying to share with us an insight that many of us are already dimly aware of: the way that we abandon our true selves, looking for something to satisfy our appetites for physical pleasures, while what we are really looking for is God, who is already dwelling within us. When we look to the world of the senses, we find traces of God but not the true reality. When we return to our true selves (not the self we try to be for other people, to impress them, or to win their affection), we realise that we are coming home. God never leaves us. But how often we lose sight of him!

Augustine works his way through the five physical senses one by one. He shows how God turned those senses away from their old sinful direction, and how they can be ways for God to reach us, despite our best efforts to bury our true selves and run away and hide from him (Genesis 3:10). There is real and poignant regret in the way he stresses how late he came to this realisation – and yet it was not *too* late. With God it is never too late. People are ready when they are ready. And, as Augustine remarks elsewhere in *Confessions*, as the creator of time, God is not subject to time. So 'too late' is an idea that has no meaning in the realm of divine love. That is a very encouraging thought for Christians!

So 'Beauty' is the first way Augustine expresses his insight into God. The gods of the Greeks and Romans were sometimes thought of as being beautiful (for example, Apollo or Venus) and occasionally were imagined as unattractive (for example, Vulcan). But their beauty was only a matter of appearance; it had nothing to do with their inner reality, their essence or their being. Thinking of God as beautiful in this way was as surprising as the Jewish insight in the Old Testament into how God loves his people and cares for them, rather than treating them like slaves whose only purpose is to serve him. So to describe God as Beauty is unexpected, and quite a change from the ways we find God being described in the Bible, where he is more likely to be Shepherd, King or Judge. But it is still completely authentic as a Christian viewpoint. What could possibly be more beautiful than God himself?

This passage, then, deserves to be called 'poetry' because Augustine is summoning every power of expression he can to try to put into words the nature and effect of God. Our God calls to us, dazzles us, makes us breathe in his truth like heady perfume; he is sweet to our taste, and even the lightest touch from him sets us ablaze.

Another way in which Augustine talks about God is more familiar to us from how God is described in the Bible: as Light. 1 John 1:5 tells us, 'God is light and in him there is no darkness at all.' And John 1:9 says of Jesus, 'The true light, which enlightens everyone, was coming into the world.' Not long after his love song to God as Beauty, Augustine addresses God as Light in more words of power and intense conviction:

> O Light which Tobit [one of the Israelites] saw, when – his own eyes blinded – he used to teach his son the way to live, and walked ahead of him, never straying, on feet of love!

And Isaac saw that Light too – though old age had encumbered and clouded his physical eyes – when he was deemed worthy not to bless his sons by the act of recognising them, but rather to recognise his sons by the act of blessing them.

So too did Jacob see the Light. When the sight of his eyes was hampered by great age, he shed radiance from a heart shining with light upon the tribes of a people yet to come, which was foreshadowed in his sons. With mystical insight he stretched out his hands and laid them upon his own grandsons, the children of Joseph – not in the way their father tried to correct him, outwardly, but as he himself perceived, inwardly.

Such is the true Light, and it is One, and all who see and love it are one.

What he is describing here is that other light, which we have already encountered in his description of his first vision – not ordinary daylight, but divine light. It is the inner light that guides us in such a way that we do not need physical vision. It is the light that guided God's people from the beginning and is guiding us still. By referring to Tobit, Isaac and Jacob, Augustine shows us that there is continuity between the past and present, so we can trust in that same Light for the future. We Christians are united by the Light that we see and love.

The third insight is also strongly biblical, and perhaps the most fundamental of all. I recall a Christian writer who said that it doesn't matter how lovely the story and message of Christianity may be (and they certainly are); none of it matters at all unless they are *true*. And the third insight is into God as Truth. As Jesus said, 'I am the way, and the truth, and the life' (John 14:6):

O Truth, light of my heart: do not let my darkness speak to me! I have deviated towards earthly things, have fallen into shadow: but from here, even from here I have truly loved you.

I wandered from the path: and then remembered you.
I heard your voice behind me, calling me to come home:
but I only just heard it over the outcry of the unquiet.
And now, look! – I am returning now, hot and thirsty
to drink at your fountain; let no one stand in my way:
let me drink from it, and hereafter let me live.
Let me not be my own life: from my own self I have lived badly.
To myself I was death: but in you I begin to come to life again.
Converse with me, commune with me:
I have believed in your holy books and their words are full of
   mystery.

Of these three poetic passages I have shared here, with their key insights into God's nature, this is the one that appeals most strongly to me. Partly this is because I have committed my life, through preaching and teaching, to what the Bible calls 'speaking the truth in love' (Ephesians 4:15). Partly it is because it expresses so well the risk we humans constantly face: to let go of God and lose sight of what matters. Most of all it is because of that simple phrase, 'Let me not be my own life.' In this world, in which people are allowed, even encouraged, to think of themselves as the centre of their own universe, those few, simple words express that visionary truth that comes to us through prayer – at the top of a mountain, beside the sea, in a quiet church – that we are both infinitesimal and yet of ultimate value. True happiness comes to us through letting go of our self, not from centring everything upon ourselves. How true it is, too, that those who lose their life will find it (Matthew 10:39).

One final passage in this chapter remains to be revealed. Unlike the previous three, where God is made known to us by means of an image, in this one Augustine simply speaks the truth from his heart, the words of love and trust spilling out of him as he tries to do justice to his feelings of love for the God who is his constant companion and friend on this journey of faith:

I beg you, God, do not keep silence towards me. You speak truth in my heart: you are the only one who does so. I will go into my room and sing songs of my love for you, uttering in groans what I cannot put into words as I continue my pilgrimage. I call to mind the heavenly Jerusalem and lift up my heart as it yearns for her – Jerusalem my native land, Jerusalem my mother. Above her you hold sway, you enlighten her – her Father, protector, spouse, her pure and powerful delight, her unshakeable joy. And you do all these things at once because you alone are the highest and true Good. I shall not give up until you bind up all that I am, from my deformed state of disintegration, into the peace of our most dear mother; and refashion me, and establish me forever, O my God, my mercy.

Ten years before he wrote those words in *Confessions*, Augustine had struggled with his feelings and bodily needs and finally accepted that, for him, life as a partner, a lover, even a husband, were no longer an option. At the time he had dreaded taking the next step, because he feared how much he would miss physical relationships and closeness. He had feared failure, because all the time he had been imagining that what was required was a massive effort of will, a heroic level of self-denial. But in the end, it was not effort and will that made the difference; it was love. Love got the better of him and, after that, there was no going back.

It may seem odd that Augustine didn't just get married and still become a Christian. He doesn't really explain why. He was certainly not anti-marriage! In fact, he even wrote about the goodness of marriage and human love, to challenge the idea, common among many Christians at the time, that living a celibate life somehow made you a better Christian. Whatever the reason, Augustine made the decision that his life belonged to God and God alone. And he never gives the slightest sign of regret. He had found an inner peace in serving God that no human companionship or affection could ever provide and, as far as he was concerned, that was that.

Augustine remained a man of many passions, but from the time of his conversion, the passion was channelled into serving God and helping others to find the divine Beauty, Light and Truth. We probably don't find it easy to express our love for God in such ecstatic terms as Augustine used, but when we read him we discover that we don't need to do so, because he has put our deepest feelings into words for us. Our best response to that is deep joy and profound gratitude. Augustine was not perfect; he had his faults and weaknesses, and becoming a Christian did not wipe them away. We are who we are, and it is for our unique individual selves that God loves us. And that is why he calls us to come home.

Perhaps we are also not as determined as Augustine was to persist in prayer. But we can surely all recognise in Augustine's life that same hunger for God that beckons to us – that desire to know God's goodness and mercy. And surely we can all find our own story in the way Augustine describes how he experiences God as both present and absent, speaking and silent. It is part of authentic Christian prayer that it is such a mixture of silence and speech. Without the silence, the sounds would make no sense.

Bible passage for reflection

The sun shall no longer be
   your light by day,
nor for brightness shall the moon
   give light to you by night;
but the Lord will be your everlasting light,
   and your God will be your glory.
Your sun shall no more go down,
   or your moon withdraw itself;
for the Lord will be your everlasting light,
   and your days of mourning shall be ended.
Your people shall all be righteous;
   they shall possess the land forever.

They are the shoot that I planted, the work of my hands,
    so that I might be glorified.
The least of them shall become a clan,
    and the smallest one a mighty nation;
I am the Lord;
    in its time I will accomplish it quickly.
ISAIAH 60:19–22

Here are words that express the beauty, wonder and glory of God. The prophet imagines a time when the light of the sun will give way to the divine light that is God himself. Such a thing is beyond our imagining, but still the vision speaks to us. It speaks to us of the truth that God is our shepherd and our king, but beyond those human images it also declares that he is the power which makes possible our capacity to see; in other words, he is *Light*. Light is the closest thing we can imagine in our earthly experience to the pure goodness, the pure power, of God himself; it weighs nothing, it seems to have no impact or force, and yet without it our lives could not exist. When we see the splendour of light in a sunrise or sunset, its warmth and glory, we can look beyond it to the creator God who brought it into being. And we can know that beyond our powers of speech, there is an ultimate Truth and Beauty in creation – and he loves us.

Questions

1 Is it true that your heart is restless until it rests in God?
2 How would you try (if at all) to put your love for God into words?
3 Does it help us to think of God as 'Beauty'?
4 Is darkness only the absence of light?
5 How can Christians ensure that they are always making progress in their journey towards God?

Prayer

Lord God, we long to know you,
and we try our best to love you;
help us to find the beauty, light and truth
that draw us closer to you:
we must ask this of you; we must seek it from you;
we must knock at your door;
and we will receive what we ask;
and find what we seek;
while already the door stands open wide, for us to enter. Amen

9

Going deeper: learning, teaching, praying, loving

Like us, Augustine had his ideal of what Christian life could and should be; he also had the experience of real life to come to terms with, when his neat and tidy dreams and plans had to give way to messy reality. It seems to be characteristic of human beings to play with unfulfillable ideals, and then be absurdly disappointed with the real life we are given. Plenty of great thinkers and philosophers have drawn up plans for ideal societies, run according to moral rules and principles, which are supposed to provide a better vision than the kinds of societies that grow up haphazardly. None of them has ever come to anything good, perhaps because the ideals they are founded on are simply too rigid to take account of the complexity of reality. But that doesn't mean those ideals have no value. They can still do good, and they have done good, by inspiring us to think carefully about the values we prioritise and the standards we aspire to. And by giving us something to aim for or live up to.

Before his conversion, Augustine described in *Confessions* just such an ideal plan, a beautiful theoretical idea of how to live as a Christian community dedicated to wisdom. But he has enough honesty to laugh at himself for the way the fantasy crumbled in the face of practical reality:

> Many of us who were friends had animated discussions and debates, and had made up our minds to live a life of peace in some deserted place. We would strive to build up that peace

by holding in common whatever we owned, so as to forge a single family unit out of it all. In this way, through the purity of our friendship our collective assets would belong to each as individuals, and each individual thing would belong to all. We took the view that we could be about ten in number in the one community. We had decided that two of us should be appointed annually, like magistrates, to take care of all practical matters and leave the rest of us free from worldly business.

But next we started to consider whether our dear little wives would allow it – for some of us were already married, and others of us also wanted wives. So the entire plan, which we had constructed so perfectly, broke apart in our hands, shattered and was abandoned.

It is always much easier to imagine ourselves being spiritual and holy when we don't have to deal with practicalities, such as other people's needs and our obligations to them. Augustine was an idealist, certainly, but there was a strong streak of practical realism running through him, too, which allowed him to make his teaching on Christianity manageable and achievable, rather than off-puttingly difficult.

When people think of Augustine, they often have in their mind an austere, elderly man who is certainly wise and clever but not particularly warm or sympathetic. That is why reading *Confessions* is so important, so that we can understand Augustine more fully, even though it is not an 'important' work in terms of developing biblical understanding or knowledge about God. It shows us that what we know about ourselves is also apparent in Augustine: namely that the person we are on the outside, in our interactions with the world, is often very different from who we are in private, the selves we share only with God. This is something I always encourage people to reflect on and remember – that it is a mistake, which causes all kinds of unhappiness and a sense of failure, to compare the outside of other people's lives with the inside of our own life.

This fact about human nature is plainly the case at the end of *Confessions*, when Augustine weaves together the story of his own life and the story of God's plan for his creation. Augustine had done his very best, in his human foolishness, to put himself beyond God's reach, but still he had not succeeded. His life is like a test case for what is written in the first letter of John – 'If our hearts condemn us, we know that God is greater than our hearts, and he knows everything' (1 John 3:20, NIV):

> I used to be petrified because of my sins, and the burden of my own wretchedness. I had been turning it over in my heart and thinking hard about running away to be alone, but you forbade me and encouraged me, saying, 'For this reason Christ died for all, that those who live should no longer live for themselves, but for him for died for them.'

> Look, Lord! I cast my care upon you [Psalm 55:22] so that I may live; and I shall contemplate the wonderful works of your law [Psalm 119:17–18]. You know how ignorant and weak I am [Psalm 69:5]: teach me and heal me [Psalm 25:5; Psalm 6:2]. He is your only Son; in him all the treasures of wisdom and knowledge are hidden [Colossians 2:2–3], and he has redeemed me by his blood. Let not the proud condemn me, because I am thinking about what I cost to ransom; because I eat and drink it [John 6:54]; I distribute it; and, poor as I am, I long to be satisfied by him [Luke 16:21], and be counted among those who eat and are satisfied. And those who seek the Lord do praise him [Psalm 22:26].

As often when he is deeply moved, Augustine's words become saturated with scripture references. Indeed, more than this, the line between God's words to him and his words to God begins to blur, because the words he knows by heart as holy scripture become (in that miraculous transformation we Christians know so well) his own words. I have included the Bible references in this passage in brackets, so that you can see how he knew his Bible so well and prayed it so easily, that it became the natural way for him to express his spiritual feelings and insights when he talked with God about stuff that mattered to him. He goes on to explain them in more detail:

> I stir up my own feelings, and those of my readers, towards you, Lord, so that we can all declare, 'great is the Lord and supremely worthy to be praised' [Psalm 48:1; 96:4; 145:3]. I have said this already, and I shall go on saying it: 'I do this because of my love for your love.' After all, we pray, even though the Truth tells us, 'Your Father knows what you need, before you ask' [Matthew 6:8]. So we reveal our feelings towards you by confessing to you our pitiable condition and the mercies you bestow upon us [Psalm 33:22], so that you perfect in us the deliverance you have begun. Then we shall stop being pitiable in ourselves and will be blessed in you, for you have called us to be poor in spirit, and gentle, and sorrowing, and hungry and thirsty for righteousness, and merciful, and pure in heart, and peacemakers [Matthew 5:3–9]. What a lot I have told you – what I was capable of and what I wanted – because, Lord my God, you are good, because your mercy is eternal [Psalm 118:1].

The intensity of his love for God enables Augustine to look beyond mere words, and to declare what he saw as the highest truth – God's purpose for his creation, every aspect of which points to the same glorious conclusion: that God *is*, and is three-in-one, and as such is to be trusted, loved and worshipped with every particle of our being:

> Who can understand the almighty Trinity? There are not many souls that know what they are talking about when they talk of the Trinity. People may dispute and do battle over the Trinity, yet no one who is lacking in peace beholds that vision. I wish people would meditate upon the triad that is within themselves: such a triad is far not the actual Trinity, but I am referring to it as a topic for them to follow up and investigate, so that they can see how far from it they are. The triad I am referring to is that of 'being', 'knowing' and 'willing'. For I *am*

and I *know* and I *love*. Let those who can, see how there is in these three a single indissoluble life.

Right at the end of *Confessions*, Augustine draws the story to a close with another extraordinary passage in that most extraordinary book. He uses three questions, followed by three commands and then by three statements. Each group of three is meant to remind us of the Trinity, which was ultimately, for Augustine, the true depth of divine reality – not just Jesus the man; not just God the Father known from the Old Testament; and not just the Holy Spirit, the divine being at work in God's world. No one of the three predominates; each co-exists in a mystical union, coming together as the true identity of the force that governs our faith and shapes our lives and calls forth the best that we are capable of, to be offered up in his service and for his glory:

> What human being can give another the power
> to understand this?
> What angel can give it to another angel?
> What angel can give it to a mortal?

> We must ask it of you.
> We must seek it from you.
> We must knock at your door.

> This is how it will be received.
> This is how it will be found.
> This is how it will be opened.

Here, at last, is God's answer to the broken, confused man who set out in search of him. We know that we exist, because God has given us a capacity for self-consciousness; and yet we spend too much of our lives running away from who and what we are and pretending to be someone different. In such circumstances it is hardly surprising that so many people live discontented and unhappy lives. Our capacity for memory is how we form and maintain our sense of self. This is why dementia seems such a cruel and terrible illness; in robbing us of memory, it robs us of our own selves. Augustine knows nothing of modern medicine or modern science, yet he has somehow managed to perceive this truth centuries ahead of us, as we see when he remarks, almost in passing:

> I am a creature who remembers, I am a mind.

Not that he is arrogant enough to believe that he has all the answers to the meaning of life. On the contrary, he is mystified by his own human nature and is not shy about telling God so!

> So what am I, my God? What kind of nature am I? A complex and manifold life and one that is utterly incalculable. In your eyes, I have become a puzzle to myself, and this itself is my weakness.

For Augustine, and for us if we are ready and willing, God is 'doctor of our inner self'; he has 'struck our hearts with his word, and we have fallen in love with him'. He is also 'a lover of souls'. The relationship between God and us, as Augustine describes it, is intimate, passionate and powerful. It is not a dry academic exercise or a chilly effort of duty. Augustine was eager, even desperate, to love, though he didn't know where to direct that passion and eagerness:

> I was not in love as yet, but I was in love with the idea of love...
> I was looking for something to love, loving to love.

Hunger becomes a speaking image for how his desire, his appetite even, tries to be satisfied with less than God, and yet can never find fulfilment apart from God:

> Within myself I was hungry from the lack of inner food – you yourself, my God; but that hunger did not make me want to feast – rather, I had no desire at all for the incorruptible food. This was not because I was already full of such food: instead the more empty I was, the more I disdained it.

He doesn't see this just as his own personal difficulty, but as the key to understanding how human beings grow apart from God:

> We are driven by our greed for more possessions and by the hurt of losing them completely, by loving our personal possessions more than you, who are the Good of all. I was hungry and thirsty, not for your created works but for you yourself, you who are Truth, in whom is no variation nor shadow of turning. Still they kept placing before me platters laden with illusory distractions.

As we saw earlier, Augustine is sometimes full of regret for the time he has wasted: the adolescence frittered away in self-indulgence and promiscuity; the nine sterile years trying to find truth in that fake faith called Manichaeism; the encouragement from every side to turn away from God and concentrate on career success and climb the social ladder:

> I did not love you, and by separating from you I prostituted myself; and as I prostituted myself the cry resounded from every side: 'Well done, well done!' For the love of this world is a physical infidelity to you.

Those are very strong words: they give us a glimpse of his feelings of self-disgust. But even in his darkest moments he is still honest, genuine and perceptive about what makes him tick:

> My feelings of sexual desire were formed out of the perversion of my will. They grew into a habitual behaviour, something I could not live without. These quite small links joined themselves together into the bond I called my chain: it was a cruel slavery that had me in shackles.

His feelings of being pulled in two directions, one by faith, one by the world, will be familiar to many people who recognise themselves in this simple, sad description of the downward spiral into self-destruction:

My two wills – one old, the other new; one physical, the other spiritual – were in conflict with one another. By their strife they were shattering my soul. I was left in an unhappy place where I could neither endure remaining nor withdrawing. For where could my heart flee, to escape from my heart? Where could I flee, to escape from myself? Where could I get to, without ending up pursuing myself?

No wonder the pressure finally becomes unbearable, so that he cries out to his friend Alypius:

What is wrong with us? What is it that you have heard? People with no education are rising up and seizing heaven, and we, with all our learning, look! We are entangled in flesh and blood! Or is it just because they have gone first that we are ashamed to follow, or at any rate we are not ashamed *not* to follow?

It makes all the difference to us as 21st-century Christians to discover that one of the greatest Christians who ever lived was confused and conflicted about matters of faith, but always without letting go of God – or, perhaps more accurately, without God ever letting go of him. There is no shame in being honest before God; in fact, it is difficult for us to grow in faith without that kind of costly honesty. These words I find particularly powerful as encouragement to me in my Christian journey:

Sometimes my belief was relatively sturdy, sometimes rather flimsy, but I never stopped believing that you exist and that you have a care for us, even if I had no idea either what was the proper understanding of your essence, or what path led to you, or led back to you.

There are very few of us in whom those words awake no flicker of self-recognition. The unhappiness that seemed inescapable as he struggled to make sense of life is the inevitable result of spending our time pretending to be what we are not, trying to deceive others about who we really are. Not that Augustine would have encouraged us to learn to love ourselves as we are; he didn't want to encourage us to feel perpetually guilty, but he didn't want us to go too easy on ourselves either. Honesty mattered before everything else, because without the truth, we might say, there can be no way to life for any of us (John 14:6):

> What good was my intelligence to me? And all those complicated books I had disentangled without the help of any human tuition? When I was abandoning the teachings of the faith with my rotten and scandalous immorality? I was pondering such considerations in my mind, which was afflicted and weighed down with gnawing anxieties about the fear of death, and the truth I had not discovered.

When he finally let go of all the pretending and posing, the relief was exquisite:

> At last my mind was free from the gnawing anxieties of ambition and acquisition and of scratching the itch of physical desire and wallowing in it, and I started to pour out my thoughts to you, my illumination, my riches and my salvation, O Lord my God.

Conclusion

Augustine has taken us on a journey like no other. He has shown us how we can learn to be at peace with our turbulent inner selves, which are always questing, discontented and confused, by fixing our attention, both mind and heart (our thinking selves and our feeling selves), on the God who created us, redeemed us and sustains us. Augustine's words help us to make sense of this extraordinary journey, but he is too wise to think that the reality of God is confined by any words of human origin. When we have said everything that we can about God, we have to take the advice of a contemporary of Augustine, Gregory of Nazianzus, and let the words and ideas go and cleave to reverence, saying as little as possible to worship God almighty, Father, Son and Holy Spirit:

> The Trinity of one substance, one God from whom, through whom, in whom we have our being: we turned away from him, and became unlike him, but we were not allowed to die away from him. He is the origin to which we return; the embodiment of what we follow; the grace which reconciles us. He is the one by whose creating act we came to be; whose likeness formed us for unity; and whose peace keeps us together as one.

The journey, it turns out, is not (as we might have expected) a journey of *self*-discovery. Instead it is a journey of *fellowship*-discovery, *community*-discovery. In other words, we discover who we are ourselves by discovering that we belong together in the body of Christ, the church. God chooses this way to work in us, bestowing his grace on us, but always by means of the ministry of our fellow human-beings, our fellow Christians. The ultimate expression of this for Augustine was the community of faith sharing in the Lord's supper, or Holy Communion, which Christ gave to us so that the faithful can become the body on which they feed.

> God's promise will not fail, and peace will be perfected in us, as we learn to love one another, and see one another coming to be filled with God, and God becoming all in all.

Since we started this exploration of a great Christian thinker and teacher, we have shared in his experiences of the journey of faith, with all its twists and turns, setbacks, disappointments and frustrations; and with all its excitement, hope and joy, its ultimate blessing and fulfilment. It is time to leave the last word to Augustine himself, and to spare just a moment to thank God for all that Augustine achieved as a preacher, teacher and minister during his lifetime and for the help and guidance he has given us, his fellow Christians from the future he could not even have imagined. At last, the promises are fulfilled, and the vision becomes reality:

We shall have God as our common vision,
we shall have God as our common possession,
we shall have God as our common peace.
For whatever it is which he gives to us now,
he himself shall be to us, instead of the gifts he gives.
He will be our complete and perfect peace.

Bible passage for reflection

Then the angel showed me the river of the water of life, bright
as crystal, flowing from the throne of God and of the Lamb
through the middle of the street of the city. On either side of the
river is the tree of life with its twelve kinds of fruit, producing its
fruit each month; and the leaves of the tree are for the healing
of the nations. Nothing accursed will be found there any more.
But the throne of God and of the Lamb will be in it, and his
servants will worship him; they will see his face, and his name
will be on their foreheads. And there will be no more night; they
need no light of lamp or sun, for the Lord God will be their light,
and they will reign for ever and ever. And he said to me, 'These
words are trustworthy and true, for the Lord, the God of the
spirits of the prophets, has sent his angel to show his servants
what must soon take place.' 'See, I am coming soon! Blessed
is the one who keeps the words of the prophecy of this book.'
REVELATION 22:1–7

There is a vision set before us in the last book of the Bible, of beauty
and splendour beyond our imagination. It is a vision of light and
glory, but also a promise of healing and hope. The damaged selves
we bring to God are restored to wholeness; it is not the case that the
suffering we have endured in our lives leaves no mark. Whether we
inflicted that damage through our own sin or foolishness or whether
it came upon us without our action or fault, it still leaves a mark,
That is also the ultimate proof that Jesus Christ was truly and fully a
human being – even after the resurrection, when he ascended with

power and glory, his hands still bore the imprint of the nails. We are what life has made us, for good or ill; and we are what we have chosen to be. So we should choose wisely. We should choose life in all its fullness (John 10:10).

Questions

1 Why do you think Augustine can still speak so powerfully to Christians today?
2 What (if anything) will you take from your reading of this book to enrich your relationship with God?
3 Why do some people seem to think the Bible is boring and faith is dull, when from the inside it means everything to us?
4 Is the church (the body of Christ, the fellowship of Christian people) a help in our pilgrimage of faith or is it a hindrance?
5 God has touched us. Do we burn for his peace?

Prayer

Lord God, you have called me to know you and to serve you.
When I succeed, let me hear your voice proclaim,
'Well done, good and faithful servant.'
When I falter, and forget, and fail,
reawaken my first love, and call me back to your side,
where I may find rest, and know at last
the peace that passes all understanding.
Through Jesus Christ our Lord. Amen

Further reading

My own translation of *Confessions* is in two volumes, and comes with the original Latin:

- Augustine, *Confessions, Volume I: Books 1–8*, edited and translated by Carolyn J.B. Hammond (Harvard University Press, 2014).

- Augustine, *Confessions, Volume II: Books 9–13*, edited and translated by Carolyn J.B. Hammond (Harvard University Press, 2016).

Among the best single-volume translations are:

- Augustine, *Confessions*, translated by Henry Chadwick (Oxford World's Classics, 1986).

- Augustine, *Confessions*, translated by Maria Boulding (New City Press, 1997).

Henry Chadwick has also written *Augustine: A very short introduction* (Oxford University Press, 2001), which does exactly what it says on the cover.

I also recommend Peter Brown, *Augustine of Hippo: A biography*, revised edition (University of California Press, 2000).

Turned by
Divine Love

Starting again with God and with others

JOHN STROYAN

This book, the fruit of prayer, theological reflection and varied human experience, evokes fresh praying and thinking about all the key relationships in our lives, beginning with God. Drawing on the rich Christian traditions of both east and west, it speaks of theology and spirituality, to the head and the heart. It is a book of hope, encouraging us all to make a fresh start with God and, entering more fully into the relationship of love to which he invites us, to go out and to witness to this love.

Turned by Divine Love
Starting again with God and with others
John Stroyan
978 0 85746 750 8 £9.99

brfonline.org.uk

HOW THEY CHANGED THE WORLD

Paul W. Barnett

The more we understand biblical characters like the apostle Paul in their specific situations and time, the more we will be able to apply biblical principles to today's church, its leaders and its mission – transforming and enriching the way we do church today. *Paul and His Friends in Leadership* examines the apostle's critical relationships with key people, illustrating his humanity, faith, confidence in God and his leadership qualities. This novel approach, by an expert in the New Testament, will encourage us to reflect on leadership in the church today and help us to see how crucial authentic relationships are to our contemporary mission.

Paul and His Friends in Leadership
How they changed the world
Paul Barnett
978 0 85746 544 3 £7.99

brfonline.org.uk

Transforming
lives and communities

Christian growth and understanding of the Bible

Resourcing individuals, groups and leaders in churches for their own spiritual journey and for their ministry

Church outreach in the local community

Offering two programmes that churches are embracing to great effect as they seek to engage with their local communities and transform lives

Teaching Christianity in primary schools

Working with children and teachers to explore Christianity creatively and confidently

Children's and family ministry

Working with churches and families to explore Christianity creatively and bring the Bible alive

parenting for **faith**

Visit **brf.org.uk** for more information on BRF's work

brf.org.uk